GROUNDED
ELAINE BROWN

A LION PAPERBACK

Copyright © 1982 Elaine Brown

Published by
Lion Publishing
Icknield Way, Tring, Herts, England
ISBN 0 85648 429 6
Albatross Books
PO Box 320, Sutherland, NSW 2232, Australia
ISBN 0 86760 358 5

First edition 1982

Printed and bound in Great Britain
by ©ollins, Glasgow

Grounded

'The curtains were drawn across the frosty winter's
evening. Candles threw dancing shadows against the
pale ceiling. A carol was playing. Coloured lights
blinked from the tree ...

    Les walked in at 6 p.m.

    "I've been paid off," he said.'

At forty-seven Les Brown was an experienced pilot.
When he lost his job, the bottom dropped out of his
world. His wife Elaine kept a diary of the events
that followed, the effects of unemployment on her
husband, herself and the family. Her book will strike
a chord with the many who now share this bitter
experience.

This is a moving human story, transparently honest.
Sadly, disappointments and frustrations are common
experience. What makes this book special is its
warmth, its humour and its faith.

Les and Elaine Brown and their three teenage
children live in an Aberdeenshire village close to
Dyce airport in Scotland. The author's delight in this
beautiful part of the country adds flavour to her
writing. This is her second book for adults. The first,
The Secret of Life, was published by Lion in 1981.

Preface

I would never have chosen to write this book.
It has come about because others suggested
that I do so. They have helped me to
recognize that our present difficult
circumstances present an opportunity —
even a responsibility — to share what has
happened, and by sharing perhaps to draw
alongside others in similar straits.

This 'record of an unemployment' has been
hard and exacting to write. We have no
quick solutions or easy ideas to offer — only
the growing certainty that there *is* God-given
value in such unwelcome circumstances, and
that this will far outweigh and outlast our
present bewilderment.

This book is also a record of the kindness
shown in many different ways by a wide
group of friends, known and unknown. We
hope that they will recognize themselves in
its pages and sense the deep gratitude we
feel.

Elaine Brown

A Page from the Diary

The curtains were drawn across the frosty winter's evening. Candles threw dancing shadows against the pale ceiling. A carol was playing. Coloured lights blinked from the tree ...

Les walked in at 6 p.m.
'I've been paid off,' he said.

His temporary job had lasted since June. We have been grateful for it, even though labouring came hard after sitting at the controls of an airliner. Now it's over. Les won't have to get up early and go off to work over the holiday week. He'll be home to share the celebrations with us.

I could only think of this as I put plates of food on our candlelit supper-table. And I am still grateful.

It is Christmas Eve and the blow is somehow softened ...

Flashback
In the summer of 1964, a few months after our marriage, Les and I left Britain to begin work in East Africa. Les's flying training was soon put to the test operating light aircraft in remote areas for a mission group called the Missionary Aviation Fellowship. And I learnt such unfamiliar skills as book-keeping and radio-monitoring, as we needed to keep in close contact with the aircraft. Many guests also came and went, so there were few dull moments: fewer still when our daughter, Rachel, joined the family, to be followed three years later by her twin brothers, Stuart and Murray.

By this time Les was able to take on more responsibility in the programme, his aviation experience increasing as he tackled numerous different flying situations. In Britain he had handled larger aircraft, a contrast to single-engined operations over rugged terrain, with weather often unpredictable and navigational aids minimal. Les's lean frame grew even thinner and Rachel would giggle as she traced the crinkles on daddy's face with her small inquisitive fingers.

Then, in September 1974, after ten years abroad we began to sense a change of direction in our lives. Ill-health, schooling problems, and serious political instability all played a part in our return home.

It was as well we did not know the details of what lay ahead. For the following two years proved more difficult than any we had experienced abroad. Adjustments to a new home and school, surroundings and culture, took several months and proved particularly painful for our children. But the hardest part of all, to our surprise, was adjustment to new work. Les began a quite different job as soon as we returned. But the decision to leave aviation proved unwise. He just did not fit into this new work situation. We tried something else — still unrelated to flying because no such openings were available — and found ourselves struggling with yet more problems.

The long hot summer of 1976 dragged on, as arid and irksome as our circumstances. We believed in God. We had experienced his marvellous care and provision for us in the years abroad. We were confident that he has a purpose for our lives. So what was God trying to show us through all this? What was he *doing*?

Just a month later, we began to see. Les had been trying hard to obtain a job in flying and was at last offered a first officer's position on Dakota aircraft in Scotland, at Aberdeen. The work seemed as secure as the expanding oil industry with which it was associated. And so we moved from south to north — cat, pot-plants, furniture and all — and quickly settled into attractive rented accommodation in an Aberdeenshire village, just twelve miles from Dyce Airport. It was a tremendous relief for Les to have permanent, satisfying employment in aviation once again — and we felt happy and content. What was more, Les was back in his own home-country. We had come to a smooth, beautiful stretch of the pathway through life!

In time, Les obtained higher qualifications and was promoted to captain with the company. I shared his pleasure as career goals were reached, and felt proud as I watched my husband leave for work in his smartly-cut black uniform (usually covered with a coat so that neighbours would not notice the four gold bands on his jacket sleeves!). The company subsequently withdrew from Dyce, but that did not affect us much. By then Les had obtained alternative work — still as a captain — with an expanding local group which operated larger turbo-prop aircraft.

And so our second year in Scotland ended. We both felt grateful for God's goodness. It was easy to thank him together on the last evening of the year.

Part One
The Gathering Storm

Month 1

We began the year thinking that our hardest days were over. There was so much to appreciate and enjoy! We had no inkling of the gathering storm as January became February, taking us eagerly on towards spring.

How could we have known?

The first hint came one ordinary Thursday ...

Thursday 28 February

Les isn't happy about the way his six-monthly 'Base Check' (a compulsory six-monthly flying exam) went last week, even though the examiner passed him after the hour-long flight.

Dyce Airport 'operations' rang before breakfast. Headquarters had telexed from England: Would Les travel down as a *passenger* on today's early flight? It meant cancelling his scheduled programme flying. Why did HQ staff need to see him so suddenly? I spent the day puzzling over their summons, and busied myself around the house by way of distraction. Why not start spring cleaning?

A mischievous wind was soon wrapping the dripping net curtains round and round my spider-web washing-line.

Supper time came and went. No word from Les. The youngsters thought Dad was busy with his usual

flying programme. The phone rang as I was cleaning
the last greasy pan.

'I'll be back on the late flight.'

Nothing more. I listened for the car around
10 p.m. Soon I heard the familiar brake squeak. Les
walked slowly in. He looked completely spent. What
had happened? Why did the boss want to see him? It
was hard for Les to have to tell me all about it. Not
that his anguish showed. It didn't need to.

He went straight to the main office on arrival.
They explained that his Base Check results, coupled
with subsequent in-flight observations by a senior
pilot, were unsatisfactory. As a result he would now
be flying as first officer instead of captain for an
unspecified period. He would also need to return to
HQ for training and a further Base Check next week.
Until then he's suspended from ordinary programme
flying.

'In other words, I've been demoted,' Les said
quietly.

That stark statement of fact hurt. I felt it for *him*
with a pain which cannot be expressed in words. Yet
he has taken the blow so meekly. That makes it
harder still.

Tonight the happy, predictable pattern of our lives
has been overshadowed. Cold fear creeps in. Is this
the first ominous hint of an approaching storm? Does
Les sense it, too?

He sat by the fire while I heated the cocoa. Then
we read this evening's Bible verses, prayed briefly
together as usual, and went to bed. It was all rather
mechanical. My thoughts were elsewhere — I'm sure
God understands. Les and I haven't talked much
together. I just said:

'Never mind, you'll soon be back were you were
again!'

If only I could *know* that's going to be true. Yet
we're still in God's hands — safe. This fact is a
refuge as the day ends.

Shall we sleep as easily tonight? The wind is cold now, troubling the trees along the nearby river-bank, turning our washing-line round and round on its creaking pole. Les's colleagues are bound to wonder why he doesn't turn up for the early flight tomorrow. When they know the facts, will they be understanding?

Friday 29 February

What shall I *do* with this day? — my first thought as I woke from a deep sleep. Les must have asked himself the same question. For me there were the ordinary things — shopping in the village, ironing those net curtains, making shepherd's pie for supper. Even writing another small section of my book (*The Secret of Life*).

I could have made it quite a different day by suggesting a drive, or a bike ride together. I almost did. Then I realized Les would prefer things to carry on as usual. He's given the car a good once-over (I wish we had a garage; the rust problem is worse than ever) and is planning to finish fitting the new PVC seats to our kitchen and bathroom chairs.

The urge to share my thoughts with someone else was so strong, I cycled round to Anne's. Just the person one longs for on such occasions. She said little, knowing she didn't need to. But she gave me all I wanted — a listening, sympathetic ear, and the immense comfort of knowing the burden is now shared. She and Pete will pray, I know. That means so much when my own prayers falter.

The youngsters were bursting with happy weekend plans this evening. Stuart asked if Dad would be flying tomorrow.

'No,' Les said. 'I've failed my Base Check, so I need to do some right-hand-seat flying for a while. It means going down south next week for a bit of training first.'

The three of them were silent, expressions unchanged, facts sinking in.

'How long will you be gone?' Stuart asked.

'Will you be a captain again soon?'

He's told his school pals about his Dad's work. I suspect that quite a lot of competitive boasting goes on. How much does a boy's respect from his peers depend on his father's job?

Month 2

Saturday 1 March

Mornings steadily lighter now. There was bright
sunshine this morning, warming the cold black
beeches on the far bank of the Don. 'Old Nog', our
local heron, was fishing from his usual flat rock,
grey-white feathers preened to perfection. Such
elegance! But let a couple of crows mob him during an
upstream flight and you should hear his language!

The twins set off on a five-mile cycle ride to
Inverurie swimming-pool this afternoon. Rachel was
working up her new clientele, supplementing her
pocket money by selling beauty aids in the
neighbourhood. Les and I were alone at home. He
fetched a duty jacket and sat slowly unpicking two
gold bands from each sleeve. I wanted to weep as I
watched him. I longed to put my feelings into words
but said nothing. In moments like this, I think Les
prefers unspoken sympathy.

Mother phoned as usual this evening. I explained
the facts of the situation. It must have been a shock.
She'd been so pleased about Les's recent promotion.
But her response was one of immediate practical
concern.

'Things will probably go well next week,' I assured
her. 'And then he'll soon be operational again.'

It was hard for Les, sitting close by, to hear me

having to tell the family. The youngsters seem automatically aware of the need for consideration. The twins brought liquorice allsorts for Dad this afternoon. They know he loves them, particularly the round coconut kind.

Sunday 2 March

We walked over the hill to morning service at the kirk. Snowdrops carpeted Elsie's garden. The same familiar form of service, same magnificent window above the table, same people, greetings, smiles. The same God.

A curry lunch, then instead of the planned tramp up Benachie we took Les to Dyce. The runways were quiet, but the youngsters were wide-eyed nonetheless. They never tire of airports. We saw Les off on the company's southbound flight. It must be hard for him to watch his colleagues take up their flight-deck positions. Then we drove back for high tea. Rachel pleased her brothers by making a huge pile of pancakes.

Les is down in England now, sitting in some hotel bedroom. He expects to re-sit the Base Check before Saturday. It's late. The youngsters put things ready for school tomorrow and prayed as usual around the fire.

'Please God, help Daddy when he's flying. And when he's lonely too,' Murray requested.

Now the three of them are asleep. Easy, worry-free sleep. The room is empty, silent. And I am a turmoil of 'whys?', 'if onlys', 'what nexts?' It's worse when I'm alone. I force myself to open the Bible and read as we'd do together if Les were here. I force my mind to concentrate, absorb, accept. It's a battle.

Paul says, in the letter to the Romans, chapter 8: 'We know that in all things God works for good with those who love him, those whom he has called according to his purpose.'

What do his words mean? Are they still true, even when the 'good' is far from apparent?

Later

James, a first officer with the company, phoned. I tried to explain what's happening. He'd guessed something was up.

'Come round! Let's talk. I'll get Mary to put the coffee on.' (They are only a few doors away.)

Mary welcomed me with a small glass of much-prized hazelnut liqueur. Then she served coffee and chocolate biscuits. Their thoughtfulness was a real comfort. We sat around the table talking about Les's position.

'Everyone dreads those regular Base Checks,' James pointed out.

'God must have seen this coming. And he must know where it's going to end,' I said, almost to myself. Putting it into words helped me feel it was true.

I realized as I walked home — oyster-catchers shrieking overhead — that God had brought 'good' to me this evening through James and Mary. Their gift of a few hours in the midst of a busy programme (Mary is revising for university exams) has brought new strength to cope.

Friday 7 March

Golden crocuses are budding in the front flower-bed. Skeins of wild geese fly north across the sky, their calls a strange, magnificent sound! Fat maternal ewes in the field beyond the river plead for 'neeps' (turnips) — a tractor delivered a load at midday.

Tonight Murray has been working hard on the fibreglass hull of his latest model yacht. He needs advice from Dad. Hopes to start buoyancy trials on the river this weekend. The bathtub is now inadequate!

The phone rang at 7. Les.

'Can you meet me off the late flight? More later.'

The youngsters weren't inclined to go to bed, but at last I set off alone for Dyce. As soon as I caught sight of Les, I knew something was wrong.

'I failed the Base Check as first officer,' he said as we drove home.

I didn't grasp the real significance of this, its implications for Les's future as a pilot. All I felt was a longing somehow to take the force of this further blow for him. But it's not possible.

Years ago a friend asked, 'Could you endure having to stand helpless while someone you love suffers?' It seemed an irrelevant question then, as we sat drinking coffee together in a beautiful Nairobi garden. Now I'm beginning to understand. We can't always rush in and relieve. Sometimes we have no choice but to trust a person we love entirely to God's care. It's hard. It goes against every instinctive reaction. Yet it has to be, if 'letting go' is a part of love.

The company have offered Les another attempt at the Base Check on Monday. But he doesn't want to accept.

'It's not right to take the examiner's time, or allow them to bear the expense of operating an aircraft for an hour when I'm still likely to fail.' He reckons he's finished. He will resign ...

Monday 10 March
We've lived with this dilemma all weekend. I felt I must reason with Les.

'They're willing. Surely a re-sit would be right?'

At last he agreed to try — mostly, I think, to please me. There was a spare seat on this morning's southbound flight, so he left after early breakfast. My thoughts kept turning to that flying test, particularly at lunch-time. It was scheduled for around midday, after a couple of warm-up circuits.

Rain fell steadily all day, the banisters now draped with damp clothes. The cat was disgruntled at having to go out, and ventured no further than the overhanging eaves. The robin sang contentedly just above her. Benachie's granite peak was hidden all day by thick white mist. I cycled to and from the village shops, head down against the rain. The crocuses, splashed with mud, were bravely bearing up.

'When's Dad getting back?' Rachel asked, the minute she got in from school — long wet hair sticking to the bomber jacket she insists on wearing.
'Maybe on the late plane.'
'Can we come with you to meet him this time?'
'Only if he makes the earlier flight.'

Les phoned at supper time. His voice sounded weary. He'd failed, and was on his way home – the plane due in around 8. The youngsters were immediately excited at the thought of another trip to Dyce. At the airport they bought funny postcards and tried having their pictures taken at a cheap photo booth, while I waited at the arrivals barrier, smiling a little at their fun.

But they were silent most of the time as we drove home, sensing the weight on Dad's mind. Did I make matters worse by urging Les to try that re-sit? But if he hadn't, he might have regretted not taking the opportunity. It was hard, but I think it was right.

Later, I tried to comfort Les as we sat by the fire, rain still flinging itself against the window. But my words sounded clumsy, inadequate. There is more empathy in silence, a caring touch.

Tuesday 11 March
Now, a day later, the significance of the situation is sinking in. It's slow, relentless, inescapable. For Les the sense of failure is hardest of all. What's he thinking, as he digs the garden for potato-planting, or scrapes the old varnish off that dining-room chair?

'Why did this happen after years of competent flying abroad?'
'Why now, just when I'm used to the new aircraft?'
'What am I going to *do*?'

'I've got a hang-up,' Les said as we sat together over a soup-and-sandwich lunch. 'I'm stuck in a psychological rut. I can't pass this test however many times I try.'

His confidence has been crushed. I want to rush in and 'make it better' — but I can't. I can only offer my support — in simple practical ways, keeping things going as normally as possible here at home.

Les has resigned from the company.

'It has to be,' he told me.

He spent a long time wording the letter and completed it in time to catch this afternoon's post.

I can't believe we've reached this point — that there's no way round it. It's such a drastic step. Yet I must accept that Les has to take it. I've been trying to tell myself that Les's skill and experience will soon get him a new job. He has so many contacts. Former colleagues will be able to advise, even help him get back in. It's not uncommon for pilots to fail a Base Check, and he feels sure that, once he shakes off this hang-up, he'll succeed. He failed on different points at every re-sit — which shows exam nerves rather than incompetence. And each procedure had been successfully carried out so many times before.

But as I watched him set off for the village with that letter, I wanted to object. Why did it have to come to this? Why does God allow the pleasure of fulfilment and success one year, then sudden failure the next? I remembered a minister once telling me, 'The answer to why is often wait.' Perhaps time will bring us a new perspective. But it was disturbing to feel the seeds of bitterness putting down their first small evil root.

'Search me, O God, and know my heart. Try me and know my thoughts ... lead me in the way ever-lasting.'

This evening, over supper, we explained our situation to the youngsters. It's less than a fortnight since Stuart asked, 'Will Dad be a captain again soon?' Now each of us is trying to grasp and accept Les's straightforward statement:

'I've handed in my notice. I shan't be flying with the company again. Now I must look elsewhere for work.'

Stuart immediately burst out with 'Whatever shall I say to my friends at school?' and I realized once more how vital Dad's position is to his own twelve-year-old prestige.

'You don't have to say anything,' Les told him, 'unless they ask. Then just give them the facts. No need to cover up.'

Rachel saw the blow most from her father's point of view. She put an arm round his neck, and said, 'Let's go back to Ethiopia, Dad. You'd soon get a flying job there, wouldn't you?'

There was a long pause.

'No, not now,' Les answered slowly. 'Those flying days are over. And anyway, we couldn't uproot you from school with O-levels this year, could we?'

She frowned, trying to understand. Murray said nothing. He is the silent-sympathy type.

After supper Les enjoyed a rough-and-tumble on the floor with the boys. Shrieks of laughter, between grunts and groans! I love to watch and listen. It's so important to switch off the problem and turn on the fun, even if only for a little while. Dad's capacity for play has really helped the youngsters this evening.

Paul phoned from England around 9 p.m. Les asked how things were going for him with the airline. He's been a first officer on jets for some months now. When he heard our news, Paul was full of kindly concern for Les, straight away offering suggestions. Les jotted down details of companies which are recruiting at present. It looks hopeful! So a hard day has ended on a happier note. Paul has a way of phoning at just the right moment.

Friday 14 March
Today's early post brought a letter from the company accepting Les's resignation. It was formal but understanding. Les will not be required to work the official three-month's notice, although pay cheques

will continue — also other privileges such as the 90 per cent reduction on air fares for us all. We'll still be able to visit Holland over Easter!

'So the pressure's off, as far as money goes, for a little while,' I commented as Les filed the letter away in his 'employment' folder. 'That will certainly help.'

He drew up a list of local flying companies and began to phone round, getting a general picture from friends on the admin. side first of all. They were surprised to learn about his problem, and I heard Les having to answer their many 'Whys?'

By lunch-time he'd made half a dozen calls and had numerous details listed on the phone pad.

'What sort of job might you get?' I asked as we sat over lunch. (I bought cream doughnuts at the bakery this morning for a treat!)

'Quite a few possibilities,' Les told me. 'I'll steer clear of anything which is single-crew though. I don't fancy an operation like that up here — especially in winter when the weather gets bad. But that still leaves me a considerable choice. I'll write in and apply to one or two operators this afternoon.'

He sounded cheerful. It's a good time of year for openings. Companies are about to introduce summer timetables and need additional crews.

'Though they may have got them all lined up already,' Les pointed out.

I baked for the weekend while he typed his applications. Then the youngsters ambled in from school. Murray licked the scrapings of cake mixture from the bowl while Rachel explained how she's *got* to go to Aberdeen tomorrow to buy a swimming costume and sandals, ready for the summer.

'Maybe trousers,' she added. 'And I'll look out for a nice sweat-shirt as well!'

Les glanced up from his letters and sighed. But there was a twinkle in his eye.

'Whatever next? *Girls!* Glad I've only got one of them!'

'Well, I'm going to pay for it all myself,' she retorted. 'Out of my earnings. You won't have to fork out for me much longer.'

There was something deliberate about Rachel's answer. It was her blunt teenage way of saying, 'I want to be one less worry for you.' We got the message.

Sandra came across the road to borrow a stencil. She's typing the village news-sheet this month. We chatted briefly on the doorstep.

'I've seen Les around a lot lately,' she said. 'Anything wrong?' (I wonder how many times she's puzzled over that fact this past fortnight. Are the rest of our neighbours asking the same question?)

'He's lost his job,' I told her, then realized that was not quite true. 'At least, he's handed in his notice.'

Sandra looked surprised.

'But I thought he was doing so well?'

'Yes, he was,' I stalled. Then I explained about the failed Checks and the inevitable outcome.

'Oh, I *am* sorry,' she sympathized. 'But I'm sure he'll soon get something else. Bob was out of work a couple of years back. Then he got this good job on the oil rigs, and now we're better off. Anyway, I must away to finish this typing!'

I watched her go. It was chilly now, and dark. Stars were beginning to poke bright holes in the black sky. Maybe Sandra will let others round here know about our problem. I won't mind if she does. Saves me having to relate facts over and over again. Strange how I find myself needing to know that others, like her, are with us, in the thick of this. I'm not as self-contained as I like to imagine.

Later Anne phoned to ask me round for a cup of tea on Monday.

'Pete and I are praying for you both — often!' she added. They don't know how much we value this, especially now, with job possibilities in the melting-pot. I told her all about it.

'Sounds good!' she said.

Last thing tonight we stopped to thank God for

those who've thought of, or prayed for us today. It reminded me that we need to keep friends posted with news.

The cry of a hungry owl echoed through the woods as we came up to bed.

'Not much on his menu tonight!' Les muttered. Cold weather is lingering on this year, so maybe the mice have chosen to remain in winter storage for a while yet.

Monday 16 March
Spring is trying at last! We couldn't resist the invitation of bright sunshine this afternoon.

'Let's cycle round the river route,' Les suggested when lunch dishes had been cleared away.

Soon we were discovering fat buds on the chestnut trees and the first bloom of a wild daffodil. Amazing how flowers grow in unpicked abundance along the lanes up here! The scene brought back the joy of our arrival — three springtimes ago!

Tuesday 24 March
Marvellous news! A local airline has processed Les's application and they are offering him an interview at their head office tomorrow! He was just back from visiting various contacts at Dyce — this airline being one — and his face broke into smiles as he shared it all with me this afternoon. So my comment, 'You'll soon be back where you were again!' could quickly prove true. I'm over the moon!

'The fact that we're already settled in the area goes down well with prospective employers, too,' Les told me as we sat out on the back step drinking mugs of tea. He's planning to drive down to the company's head office first thing tomorrow.

'Must check the car over now!' he said, jumping up. 'And do you know where the road map is?'

It was marvellous to see Les looking so relieved and happy. Later, he got his brief-case down from the hall rack and checked through its contents. 'Mustn't forget my licence and log-book.'

Murray gave Dad's shoes a brush-up this evening, and I packed honey sandwiches for his lunch. He'll be off 'at the crack'.

Thursday 26 March

It looks good! They'll be following up references and letting Les know the score within a couple of weeks. He'll be able to re-sit his Base Check with the company, too, and although Les was frank with them about his reason for being out of work, they don't seem to anticipate problems.

Les phoned Paul tonight. (He's the one who recommended this airline and he's as hopeful as we are.) 'Sounds an interesting operation too!' he said.

School term finishes tomorrow. The youngsters are counting days to our Dutch trip. Only six to go. Rachel has packed her suitcase already.

'You'll really be able to enjoy our Easter holiday now that there's another job in the pipeline!' I said to Les. There will probably be a reply from the company waiting on the mat when we get back.

Month 3

Wednesday 2 April

A bright sunny morning. The youngsters were awake early and keen to force down the last suitcase lid. Took the cat to the cattery after our quick breakfast — then off we went! The airport had happy, exciting associations this time. Even so I wondered if Les was going to find it hard to travel as a passenger aboard his former company's aircraft. The crew gave us a warm welcome and after take-off one hostess spent a while talking with Les. I was touched by her practical concern for him.

A brief stop at Edinburgh. 'Hey, look at that suspension bridge!' Stuart yelled as we approached. Rachel tried an aerial shot of the Castle. Then a snack, en route for Amsterdam. The youngsters were given special junior hampers by the hostess. I envied them their salted peanuts and big chocolate bars! Soon on 'finals' for Schipol Airport. Nothing to be seen of the city but tower blocks. No sign of tulips! Once through formalities (it was intriguing to hear Dutch voices all around), we phoned Susan and waited for her to pick us up. Stuart carefully chose an expensive postcard for a friend.

Great to see Susan making a bee-line for us through the crowd. 'Hi, *my* boys!' she said, reminding them that they were her special responsibility when they were born at 'her' hospital in Ethiopia. We drove

out to Woerden, absorbed with new sights and
sounds all the way. Our biggest surprise was the
water! It's everywhere. Even the new housing estate
where Susan lives is criss-crossed with canals. Huge
fun for the local youngsters (Stuart's glad he
struggled all the way from Aberdeen with a large
model launch under his arm!) and a happy dabbling-
ground for numerous mallard families. Susan gave us
a typical Dutch welcome — warmest of warm — and
her home is as full of houseplants as all the rest
along this street. She served an Indonesian menu for
supper and then the youngsters found their rooms —
the twins have camp-beds up in the attic.

Saturday 5 April

'We're going to hire bikes today!' Susan announced at
breakfast. All shapes and sizes are available from a
shop beside the station. And soon we were setting off
in a row along town roads. The unfamiliar back-
pedal brakes were hard to operate. I wasn't quite
sure I'd make it through the crowded street-markets
in full swing today! I nearly collided with a young
mother carrying two children as passengers on her
bike. Before long we reached the outskirts of Woerden
and branched off into a quiet country lane bordering
a small canal. A haze of soft green hung about the
willow trees and birds were busy in the water —
ducks, swans, herons. Sheep meandered across flat
green fields and pigs snuffled their way through
clean hay in a clean farmyard. Everything was
vibrant, eager, gleaming in the warm Easter
sunshine. Further on we stopped to admire a
magnificent castle (it made our Scots ones seem very
unimpressive!) and then pedalled past a picturesque
old village. There's so much to delight us — spring
flowers, windmills, colourfully-painted window-
shutters, the clatter of clogs. Today I've been
realizing my need to be constantly open to beauty
and pleasure, even in the midst of our problems.

The youngsters enjoyed Dutch TV programmes
tonight (a rare treat, as we don't have a set

ourselves). They couldn't understand a word, but still seemed to get the gist of things. We're all glowing after that good long ride out into the country. I don't think any of us will forget the fun today!

6 April, Easter Sunday

An early breakfast. Eggs were arranged all over the table — chocolate and real ones! Susan had made plans for us to attend morning service at the Scots kirk in Amsterdam, so we were soon heading towards the city along empty roads. The air was still.

'Even Woerden's windmill isn't turning!' Rachel remarked as we left the town behind.

'We'll walk around the streets later,' Susan said, leading the way through a narrow alley to the church beyond. It was set in a small, colourful garden. We were welcomed at the door by a sidesman wearing a kilt — which made us feel at home. The small, simple building was packed already. I noticed bowls of daffodils and yellow rosebuds on each window-sill.

The organ began to play — familiar harvest music in an unfamiliar place: 'We plough the fields and scatter the good seed on the land.'

I smiled to myself, thinking the Dutch organist had got his seasons muddled.

But no, seeds *do* have a lot to do with Easter after all! The minister read Jesus' words: 'Except a corn of wheat fall into the ground and die, it abides alone ...' Straight away I realized the connection. Surely the seed must die before it can offer its gift of life? Only in dying can it live on. What an amazing picture of Jesus' sacrifice of himself for me. He dies — that I may live! So Easter Sunday becomes the glad spring harvest following Good Friday's death!'

It was a magnificent day — warm and bright, a playful breeze stirring the budding trees which stand straight and tall above each busy canal. We walked along famous streets, ate pizzas at a small Italian restaurant, then took a barge trip on the waterways.

'That's a cats' barge,' the guide told us, pointing to

a newly-painted craft. 'Only city cats are allowed on board — and the lady who cares for them.' We noticed several contented residents sunning themselves along the deck.

The day was over too soon. Murray and I caught the train back, while the rest crowded into Susan's small car. Tomorrow our holiday ends.

Monday 7 April

It was hard to know how to thank Susan for all she'd done. None of us wanted to leave this morning. The flight back was smooth and easy; almost empty, too. High above the North Sea my mind went back to that 'death of the seed' idea. Is every setback we encounter meant to be a 'dying' of some kind, so that out of it we may gain something new and important? Will Les and I find this to be true, even in our situation? Yes, but only if we *let* it become true. The 'letting' is the hardest part. It means we have to trust.

'Look! There's Aberdeen again!' Stuart cried as we cruised in, low over the harbour. On our way home we collected the cat (how she hates that posh cattery!) and stopped for groceries. Now for all those letters awaiting us on the mat!

'Yes, quite a heap!' Murray told us, pulling open the front door.

I quickly put down my bags to sort through the pile of envelopes. Anything official? Anything from that airline? It didn't look like it. I checked again. No, nothing.

'Guess it will come tomorrow!' Les said, hiding his disappointment.

The youngsters couldn't wait for our late lunch.

'*Please* can we have those luscious chocolate biscuits Susan gave us?' Rachel pleaded. There was a long cucumber, too. Susan slipped it into my basket at the last minute. She knows Rachel loves them — especially the juicy Dutch variety.

Monday 14 April

Life is lively these days. School holidays are
guaranteed to keep every mum on the hop. It's a
week since we got back from Woerden and more than
two since Les's last contact with that airline. Why
the delay?

'I'll wait and see what the postman brings this
morning,' Les said over breakfast. 'If nothing comes,
I'll phone.'

The postman was later than usual. We heard the
letterbox click at 11.30. Les picked up the three
envelopes. Mother's fortnightly letter, the telephone
bill, and an air letter from Kenya. So it still hadn't
arrived. Disappointment suddenly dulled my day. I'd
felt sure Monday's post would bring something, after
waiting all weekend.

Les put a call through to the airline's head office.
I heard him ask for the 'operations director'.

'Captain Brown here . . .' Les began. How much it
means to hear him use that title again.

I listened as I sliced up chips for lunch. There was
a long silence as Les was given some sort of
explanation. Then a sad-sounding, 'Oh, I see.' My
heart sank. I knew the outcome already. '*No* God,
how will he be able to bear such a blow?' Les put the
phone down, looking stunned. I tried to find the right
words but there weren't any. There's nothing I can
do. Nothing at all. Oh, the wretchedness of this
situation!

'Why?' I asked at last, as Les slowly sat down at
the half-laid lunch-table.

'I don't really know. He just said their crew
vacancies had now been filled.'

The twins rushed in. They'd been trying to inflate
the dinghy ready for a proposed river trip in the
afternoon.

'When's lunch? I'm dying from starvation!' Stuart
said. Chips are always acceptable in such
emergencies.

The youngsters know we like peace and quiet over
after-lunch coffee, so they left us on our own. Les and

I tried to analyse this latest setback. Had the ops. director changed his mind as a result of following up references? Will Les's hang-up with that Base Check continue to dog his footsteps? The thoughts churned round and round my mind this afternoon. The storm has broken now. And if *I* feel overwhelmed, what must it be like for Les? What are we going to do next? I'd been placing all my hope and confidence in this particular opening.

I decided to tackle the pile of ironing after supper. It gave me a chance to think. The first shock of the blow was over. I could begin to be more objective.

'Our income from that last company is still coming in,' I reminded myself. 'Six more weeks before it stops.' This gives us a good margin of time. Les will certainly have found employment by then. What a relief not to face financial worries on top of everything else! I can't imagine what having to sign on for the dole would do to Les. That really *would* be the last straw.

'No need to think about such awful things anyway,' I told myself as I folded the last sheet.

'Mum, it's ice cream night!' Murray said. I'd almost forgotten the once-a-week treat we have to cheer up dull Mondays. The van drew up outside, horn blaring. No wonder a nearby Dad calls it the 'I Scream Van'! Murray hurried out to choose our favourites — a small reminder of the plenty we enjoy on Les's quite adequate salary (£9,000 basic per annum). It helped me get things back into perspective.

Tomorrow's another day! It may well bring news of an alternative work possibility.

Tuesday 15 April
Paul phoned this afternoon, just to find out how things are going.

'I've got a day off tomorrow,' he told Les. 'So I'll catch the early flight and come up to see you!'

Les objected, but Paul is determined. Apparently the idea has been in his mind for a couple of days and he feels even more concerned about coming now that he knows the latest score.

'All right Paul, we'll let you come!' Les said.

We appreciate Paul's thoughtfulness. Les will value a chance to chat with him.

Wednesday 16 April

Still more sunshine! Along the river-bank shy wild pansies are in bloom, celandines budding. On the far side, daffodils splash the new grass with gold. Glorious time of year!

Les has been at home for six weeks now. He doesn't express his feelings but I try to imagine how irksome this must be. He's such an active person. What must it be like to wake up to a blank each morning?

We're slowly getting into a shared routine at home. I'm afraid I might be putting on him, but Les says he's only too glad to have something to do, even if it's washing dishes or operating the twin-tub. I've heard other wives say that they can't bear having a husband underfoot in the kitchen. I guess it depends on the husband. Les seems to know how to fit in, rather than take over. I'd soon protest if he tried to organize me!

We've been trying to discover the 'plusses' in our 'minus' situation. We enjoyed one yesterday.

'Let's pack up a picnic and drive along the "Lord's Throat" road!' I suggested. The sun was shining down from a gleaming blue sky, and we ate our sandwiches overlooking a quiet upriver stretch of the Don, before walking across Millstone Hill. A joy to breathe in the fragrance of all those close-growing pines!

Having Les's help around the house is offsetting the strange difficulty I'm having with my hands. I noticed it first on Friday, when I couldn't wring out the dishcloth. My fingers refused to grip. It's stupid, and annoying. This morning, making beds took longer than usual. I couldn't seem to hold the bedclothes tight enough to pull them straight. I even tried grasping a sheet with my teeth — must have looked ridiculous!

Peter and Maureen phoned around 10 a.m. They were driving out this way and would like to visit.

'Yes do. I'll have coffee ready!' I told them.

I was glad to relax with them both. Calling on us is their way of showing they care for and remember us. Peter's flying is going well. He's steadily building up hours at the airport club and hopes to get his Assistant Instructor's rating some time this summer. Les enjoyed talking shop.

Peter and Maureen set off towards Inverurie just before Les went to meet Paul from Dyce. His plane was due in around 12. Today's been a real 'visitors' day! I was just putting frozen peas into the pan when Paul walked in. It was great to see him!

'What a way to spend your day off,' I protested with a smile, 'when Joey could be enjoying you at home.'

'No, we both wanted it this way,' Paul told me. 'Nothing like a chance to sit and talk things over face to face.'

After lunch we settled into armchairs for a long chat. (Paul had to catch the late afternoon flight back to Gatwick.) It meant so much to be able to discuss our situation frankly with another pilot — someone who knows Les, too, having flown as a colleague with him in Africa. Paul confirmed the fact I've been clinging to all through these weeks. Les *is* competent at his job, well able to handle any situations which might arise. No need to doubt his ability — 'flying flows in his blood!'

'Some people have said that God might be using circumstances to show us that he doesn't want Les to fly any more,' we told Paul. 'What do you think?'

'I feel it's very important for him to get another job *in aviation*,' Paul insisted. 'Only then will his self-confidence be restored. Surely God doesn't lead us out of something he's equipped us to do by suddenly letting us fail and give up?'

I stored those words away in my mind. Paul was right.

Paul gave Les details of several other flying companies — not all local operators, though. I pushed aside a fear which has been niggling for a few days. Surely Les won't have to work away from home? Not when we're all so happy and settled up here? I don't even want to think about it.

Paul's visit has given Les a real boost. I can see it in his face. We had lots of laughs together, too.

'God seems to know exactly how to encourage us,' I commented when Les got back from seeing Paul off. He's put the list of prospective flying companies beside the phone and will make enquiries as soon as office hours begin tomorrow.

Wednesday 30 April

Is it ever possible to get used to disappointments? Each one seems as hard as the first. We've lost count of the number of phone calls Les has made since Paul came two weeks ago. Initial contact with a company usually results in an application form being put in the post. Les receives it a couple of days later, fills in details, and posts it back straight away. Then he waits for three days before following up with a phone call.

He had quite a few to make this morning, while I worked close by in our open-plan kitchen/living area. The cake tins needed filling again. They're always being raided by the boys. Talk about man-sized appetites!

Les settled himself down beside the phone, beginning each conversation so hopefully. But every one ended the same way.

'Oh, I see ... Thank you all the same ... Goodbye!'

I reached a point where I couldn't bear to hear Les saying those words. He's waited so long — with such eager expectancy — and then there's nothing but a clear-cut 'No'.

Les put the receiver down and sat in silence for a

while. Then he crossed most of the companies off his enquiry list, and put the piece of paper away.

'I think I'll follow up that Sudan possibility this afternoon,' Les said as I ladled out the soup for lunch. He paused, waiting for my response. That niggling fear intensified.

'But what would it mean?'

'Well, I'd go on my own, while you and the children stayed here. It's the only way. We couldn't uproot the youngsters at this critical stage of their education.'

His voice was gentle. He hates the thought of a separation as much as I do. To think that we're even having to consider such a step. Just two months ago it would have seemed ridiculous.

'But how long will you be gone?'

'Only a year, with plenty of home visits in between. And you and the youngsters could come out on a trip once or twice! The terms of this contract sound exceptionally good. There's the income, too. Even better than my last salary!'

He was forcing himself to look at it all in a bright light. There was no alternative. I could not bring myself to crush his efforts with a quick, blunt objection. I don't need to express my fears. Les knows they're there.

'A year will soon go by,' he tried to reassure me. 'And by then something will have turned up here again!'

In the afternoon I was out loosening hard-packed soil around new shoots in the garden. The perennials seemed glad to be released. As I worked, I struggled with my bewilderment. Hadn't we always felt it was right for all of us to be here in Scotland? And to stay together as a family, whatever the circumstances? How would Les manage out there? I'll be living in a hotel I expect,' he'd said. But what about all the lonely off-duty hours? And what would it be like operating aircraft over vast empty desert areas?

coping with an exhausting climate? or with fuel
shortages, lack of spares, few navigational aids?

Somehow it seemed all wrong. I began to wonder
how the children would accept Dad's absence. All
three are so Dad-orientated nowadays, rushing to
share successes and secrets with him the moment
they get in from school. He and the boys enjoy many
common interests — aircraft, model boats, woodwork.
How would I be able to solve a model tug's engine
problems? answer endless questions about such
things as 'displacement' and 'vortices'? or coach
them with physics and maths? It's just not *me*. True,
we'd be able to shelve some of the problems till Les
got home on a visit, but what about those which
couldn't wait? A tricky algebra question which has to
be answered by tomorrow's lesson, or bigger
headaches like a smashed electric light fitting, frozen
pipes, problems with starting the car? What then?

And these were all in the 'practical' category. I
dared not let myself imagine what it would be like
without Les's companionship and support over a long
period of time.

'We've experienced separations before,' I
reminded myself, 'but only for three weeks at the
most.'

A recent conversation with Sandra came to mind.

'I just have to live a completely different life
when Bob's away on his usual two-month stint,'
she'd told me. 'It's the only way to survive. For two-
thirds of the year he goes his way and I go mine.
During the rest of the time we try to make up for the
long separations. But it's not easy.'

Was I willing to live like that, even for a year?
Only one factor *would* make me willing — seeing Les
get a good flying job in which his shattered
confidence could be restored. Anything to see Les
back where he once was.

The sun moved round; shadows crept across our
small lawn, and it was time to go in and get the
supper. One last thought went through my mind as I
brushed the dirt off my slacks. Les needs to be sure

of my basic faith in him through all of this. Bewilderment over present circumstances must not be allowed to undermine the trust we've built up over long years together. Maybe knowing that I still have faith in him will help Les have more confidence in himself.

Month 4

Thursday 1 May

I'm finding it so difficult to move these mornings. Why? Making my legs co-operate is a slow, clumsy process. Today I was glad Les was still dozing when I got up to wake Stuart for his 7.30 bus. I'd hate him to see me. The thick stair-carpet muffled my awkward steps. No one heard or saw. That was a relief. Stuart was soon up and about, so I left him to his cornflakes and toast while Les and I drank mugs of tea upstairs. Getting back up was easier and I climbed into bed without too much difficulty. Even so, Les looked surprised.

'Whatever's wrong?'

'Oh, just stiff.'

But I know it's more than that. It was obvious, later, when I started to wash the kitchen floor. Something has gone wrong. No amount of cover-up is going to alter the fact. My fingers tried to squeeze out the cloth, but it was no good. They wouldn't work. Water lay in small pools across the floor as I got myself up on to the kitchen chair. Les was busy outside putting a coat of creosote on the back gate. (Another warm bright morning. Summer must be on our doorstep!)

I sat there for a long time, hating the thought of having to seek medical advice. But there didn't seem much choice. At first it seemed such a small, insignificant ailment, but now each day brings new difficulties — jar-lids won't turn, spoon-handles slip round while I'm trying to stir the porridge, clothes-pegs refuse to open, the breadknife zigzags off course. Taps are the worst. I can get my hand over the tops but then each finger baulks, determined not to grip or twist, and I'm thwarted. It's ridiculous, infuriating. The last thing we need around this house just now is an incompetent wife/mum. Besides, independence is my pride and joy. I delight to do what I like, when I like, how I like.

Independence? That's the most frightening part of all. To enjoy it I must be able to get around with ease, yet even that is now under threat. My feet won't operate properly. It's not too noticeable on the flat but stairs and cycling show up the clumsiness. I can't hide it any more. Not that movements hurt; they're merely all out of sequence. Guess I'm seizing up or something.

'Dear God, what can I do? Don't let me get worked up about symptoms. Show me what action to take.'

If anyone else in the family had similar problems I'd have phoned for a doctor's appointment ... so? Slowly I dialled the number. He was bound to be fully booked. But no, he would see me at 11 a.m. Jitters set in. What would I tell him? What would he say?

'Just off for some shopping!' I told Les. 'Oh, and I've got a doctor's appointment, too. A check-up.'

My hands and feet had loosened up after the morning's chores, so the cycle brakes and pedals didn't pose too many problems this time. It took about three minutes to tell the GP what was wrong. He tried me out on a few movements, then called in a colleague. The movements were repeated. They asked questions. Then one turned to the other and said 'MS?' (multiple sclerosis).

My whole world seemed to split apart.

'No, Lord. NO. Anything else. Anything. But not THAT!'

The doctor didn't realize I'd heard.

'Come and wait for the nurse to take some blood,' he said, smiling kindly and leading me towards a chair. I sat there, holding an open magazine, trying to blink back tears.

It can't be. They must have got it wrong.

The nurse was full of sympathy. Not that I said much. Fears must be kept firmly in check. I won't even tell Les. How can I? After all, the doctors don't *know* it's MS. Why worry him unnecessarily and so increase his already heavy load? The GP is going to contact a neurologist and phone me back.

Outside, the sun shone warm and bright. What was I supposed to be buying for today's lunch? supper? Posters reminded me that it's 'local elections day' so I went and voted at the school. Nearby cherry trees were lost in clouds of pink-and-white blossom. Magnificent sight!

I shopped, then cycled slowly home. I seemed to have been away for hours. Les met me half-way.

'Where've you been? I was worried.'

'Oh, voting and getting groceries.'

'But what did the doctor say?'

'He doesn't know what's wrong. Wants me to see a neurologist.'

'When?'

'Maybe next week. He'll phone.'

Thursday's always busy at home. I caught up on some letters this afternoon. Sandra called in for a 'fly cup' (local jargon for a quick cup of tea/coffee); Rachel wanted help sewing an awkward collar on her new blouse; Les was having problems with the church 'Roneo' — could I check through pages of the parish mag. for 'blanks'? It was one of those days — and I was grateful for lots to do.

Now there's the usual late-night lull. Nothing to distract my thinking. Suppressed fear surges back.

What if the doctors are right? What if I lose my independence? How could I bear to be a burden to Les? How would I care for the children? Helplessness must be the ultimate frustration.

I remember MS patients from my nursing days — stiff limbs, dimming vision, slow speech. Yet they always looked so young, fresh-faced, apparently healthy. It was an enigma to me, even then.

MS only happens to others, not to me. I'm just walking through some brief, frightening, dream experience. Maybe tomorrow I will wake up ...

Tomorrow is Friday. I must sort out jumble for Saturday's sale, fill the cake tins again, sweep the inside of the car. Maybe the flower-borders should be weeded, and sleeping-bags aired for the twins' camping trip on Saturday? It promises to be a full weekend — Ron is coming, too, some time. *Must* keep busy, make myself do things.

'One last thing, Lord. Can you take this problem away? Yes, I know you can. But *will* you? That's different. I don't yet know what you're intending for me through this. Healing? Humbling? Perseverance? Please show me.'

Saturday 3 May

Magnificent summer's day, though officially it's still only spring. A busy morning in the kitchen. Stuart's friend Julian came, so double quantities of 'Brown Bear Pudding' were called for. Ron arrived in time for coffee. It was good to see him again. He's always an 'encourager'. Rachel arranged chairs and a rug on the lawn. We didn't need much enticement to join her out there. Scarlet tulips tall and straight along the path. Susan would enjoy seeing her Dutch gift of last year in bloom.

We caught up on Ron's news from England. Sometimes we feel a bit out of touch here. Then it was time to supervise lunch. My hands fumbled as I opened the packet of custard powder, the sachet of frozen peas. They refused the pressure of slicing onions, carrots. The slow inefficiency annoyed me. I was glad Les and Ron were still outside. I didn't want to be noticed.

After lunch there was more time to relax before Ron had to leave for Edinburgh. Les had given him details about the work situation.

'Why are we getting so many "nos" on this?' I asked. 'What's God *doing*? It seems all wrong from my angle.'

Ron's the sort of person you can be straight with. It was a relief to put my feelings into words. Of course, Ron can't assess what God is doing (only *he* knows that) but he encouraged us to cling to the certainty that God has it all in hand — past, present, future. To God nothing is baffling or unexpected; everything has been anticipated, provided for. We are still safe. There is a refuge while the storm goes on.

Tonight the house was more quiet than usual. The boys were off camping on the lower slopes of Benachie. Rachel was out babysitting. My own fears about MS returned, all the more fierce for being bottled up all day. I couldn't hide the facts from Les any longer. He wouldn't want me to. I told it all — slowly, carefully, playing down possibilities. He took my problem in the same quiet way he took his own in February. Underneath I know he is shattered. For him — unless the doctors are wrong — there'll be the agony of watching a deterioration he cannot reverse or adequately relieve. The question I faced is now asked of him: 'Could you endure having to stand helpless while someone you love suffers?'

Saturday 10 May

The postman arrived earlier than usual today — eager to begin his weekend. He brought a small official envelope stamped with the hospital address. It had come. The neurologist suggested admission. Dread and relief pulled me opposite ways. The letter gave all I need to know — date, time, place to report, items required, visiting hours. So simple and precise. Trying to be attractive. If only they knew how I loathe the whole idea.

'In on Tuesday means out by Friday!' I told Les. 'Tests should only take three days.'

All week I've fought to dismiss increasing
disability. 'Can't be much. That possible diagnosis
will prove wrong. No need to worry.' Now the arrival
of the letter has plunged me back into fear. I tried
watering the carrot seeds, unravelling Murray's
fishing-tackle, oiling the bike chain — but all the
time my mind was racing ahead over a dozen
uncrossed bridges. What if they can't do anything?
Will that eventually mean a wheelchair existence?
The thought shocked me. Even simple chores like
washing a floor or hanging out washing would pose
problems. I'd go crazy. And then suppose, seeing my
struggles, kind friends offered help. Could I be glad?

What if — pernickety person that I am! —
someone else didn't do things *my* way. They might
forget to water my prize azalea three times a week; or
they might give Murray egg sandwiches in his school
lunch-box (he'd be sick!). They might not scour round
the sink every day. Stupid, silly worries; suddenly
important. Do I need the humbling such helplessness
could bring? Have little things become too big, vital,
confining? 'Nothing like incapacity to right a wrong
sense of values!' people say.

And how long will it all take? Will dwindling
muscle-power suddenly be restored and hopes raised,
only to plummet when symptoms reappear? Or will it
be a slow, steady, relentless deterioration? Oh, how I
hate the whole miserable business ...

Just now *my* problem fills the whole screen. I
haven't yet learnt to see it in perspective, laid out
alongside the far greater sufferings with which
others struggle. Maybe that will come?

Les is expecting word from the company in
Sudan any day now. He filled in an application form
several days ago.

Anne phoned: 'Can you all come to lunch
tomorrow?'

I hesitated: 'Are you sure? We're such an
invasion!'

'Yes, Pete and I have got it all planned — see you after church!'

It'll be a real day off for me!

Sunday 11 May

Les drove us to Pete and Anne's. We were met by a mouth-watering aroma of roast beef. 'Umm!' said Stuart, eyes wide.

Ten of us round their dining-table! I was impressed by such practical kindness. Would I be so ready to prepare a special Sunday lunch for five of our neighbours?

I ate slowly, hoping it wasn't too obvious. My jaw is stiff these days.

Monday 12 May

So hot! Incredible! Who says Scotland's always wet? Have I remembered everything the family will need this week?

'Let's go for a drive!' Les said this afternoon.

We set off towards Monymusk — trees bursting into leaf; oyster-catchers foraging amongst newly-sprouted grain; swifts skimming the sky. A hare crouched beneath a broom bush, and one large cream-coloured cow stood aloof in a field of steers. We were back to the village in time to pass primary children crowding out through the school gateway, socks sagging and blazers undone. The afternoon bus arrived with late papers and the driver tossed the bundle out on to the pavement opposite the newsagent's. Perfect long-practised aim! A happy afternoon together — I almost forgot that tomorrow I shall be in hospital.

Before the evening sun had quite set we walked slowly along a short stretch of the river-bank, hearing the water murmuring over rocks and seeing the sudden splash of a hungry trout. A single swan drifted downstream (its mate must be on the nest) and lambs bleated in a field near by ... I never want to lose the wonder of it all. Could such a scene ever seem ordinary?

We prayed together before bed. Les asked for healing. I want to believe that healing is possible, yet hesitate. The faith isn't there. But maybe Les's faith makes up for my lack? Jesus didn't always require faith from the *patient* before he agreed to heal.

Tuesday 13 May

Still no further word from the company in Sudan. It's hard on Les. With so few local openings he's been placing more and more hope on this possibility. But our present circumstances pose a difficulty.

'Your problem has made me wonder if looking abroad is right,' Les said.

I was alarmed to think I could spoil his chances.

'Oh no, don't let that put you off. It'll come to nothing, you see!'

Today was the day I had to go into hospital. We set off mid-morning — rolling green countryside gleaming in the sunshine; blossom weeping from trees by the city boundary. We arrived half an hour early, so had coffee together before searching for the ward. I found it harder than usual to leave Les. Being together has proved so important these past weeks. Only three days though — I'm sure I can endure that!

It's an old ward, eight beds down each side. Most patients are elderly, living out the long evening of life in their own separate worlds. Vases of daffodils and tulips everywhere. Wide views across the city — the slender spires of Aberdeen, simple and so precisely defined against the clear skies. Nothing is required of me here except endless answers to endless questions, and co-operation with every test.

The young girl in the next bed was new, too. I tried to talk to her, saying, 'I'm sure the specialist will be able to help. They're very understanding.' It sounded hollow, unconvincing.

I was surprised when Les walked in at 8 p.m. (thought he wouldn't come till tomorrow) and glad to catch up on ten hours of home news. Rachel is coping fine with the cooking. No new developments on the job front. Stuart is excited about getting into the relay for sports day. The bell rang. It was 9 already. The ward was suddenly quiet and boring. Flowers taken out. Hot drinks served. Lights dimmed. Voices, footsteps hushed. A long, strange, empty night ahead.

Thursday 15 May

Can't wait to get out tomorrow. The heat wave goes on. I'm glad the lumbar puncture test is over. 'Now lie flat for twenty-four hours, then we'll let you home!' Marvellous! How on earth do people endure ten days or more of a place like this? I never really appreciated the patient's frustration when I was nursing.

After lunch, a boring lull. The ward receptionist tiptoed in with a large pot-plant.

'For *me*? But I'm only in for tests!' I don't feel at all deserving of such gifts. It's a Peruvian violet, a bush of delicate mauve flowers, bought for me by the Bible discussion group in the village. What thoughtfulness! And sent on this hot, sticky, stay-in-bed afternoon.

'Lord, you know exactly how to cheer me up!'

I have Mary Craig's book *Blessings* for company. Not the sort of light-hearted book you're supposed to read in hospital. It's an account of Mary's struggles in caring for her four boys, two of whom were born severely handicapped (one died at the age of ten). Sounds grim, but the book's not like that. It's honest — every feeling and frustration shared. I almost wept in places; laughed with her in others. Her descriptions of visits to war refugees are very moving. Their intense suffering is laid alongside hers. *They* have not allowed it to make them bitter — neither will she. This way suffering can even become creative.

Two sentences in the final chapter I found particularly helpful:

'The value of suffering lies not in the pain of it, which is morally neutral — but in what the sufferer makes of it.'

'Man is born broken, he lives by mending; the grace of God is glue.'

God is never to be *blamed* for suffering. It's the consequence of sin, and the resulting gone-wrong world. There was also this gem: 'Too much sunshine makes a desert.'

This evening, as a night nurse dimmed the lights, I thought back over Mary's experiences. My small adversity beckons me on to creativeness. She has shown everyone that it *can be done.* Two weeks ago, I asked God to show me his intentions through this ailment — humbling? perseverance? *Blessings* is helping to provide an answer. God is showing me that any setback — illness, unemployment, failure . . . offers a choice between bitterness or creativeness; resentment or resourcefulness. Bitterness is the natural reaction; creativeness is only possible when bitterness has been recognized and rejected.

'But *how,* God? It's so hard to rise above my natural reactions!' I see now that it can come only through humbling, persevering — letting God take over, even live *in* me, so that the 'impossible' gradually becomes a reality. (I asked him then if healing was his purpose. There's no light on that yet.)

Friday 16 May

The Registrar came into the ward at 10 a.m. 'You can go home! I'm pleased to say there's no evidence of MS so far, though there are some test results yet to come.' (That's fantastic!) 'We'll be getting in touch with your own doctor.'

On the way home I shared the news with Les — he'd already read the excitement on my face.

'What a huge relief!' I laughed, wishing his enthusiasm would match mine.

'Why all these marked disabilities then?' was all Les said. Talk about a wet blanket.

Great joy to be home! The hot summer days continue. The London secretary of the company in Sudan phoned. Les's application is still being processed.

They're obviously interested. Les didn't say much in response to my optimism — he seems temporarily to have lost his enthusiasm for job-hunting.

The youngsters were just in from school: 'Hi, Mum! Better now?'

'Yes, getting along fine!' I told them, hoping Les wouldn't qualify the statement.

'Dad's still thinking about Sudan,' Stuart told me, filling me in on developments.

'Yes, and he won't take us with him,' Rachel added, wearing a hurt look.

Murray was silent, as usual.

'But we *will* go for holidays!' Stuart explained.

'Hey, does that mean lots of swimming, and seeing the pyramids, and eating mangoes?' Rachel cried, suddenly enthusiastic.

'And riding camels?' asked Murray.

'Yes, and maybe a trip to Israel as well,' Les told us. 'I could meet you in Jerusalem and then we'd spend a week or so going round all those Bible places.'

Everyone was in good spirits, the youngsters bursting with happy plans. They were almost there already.

'Wait till I tell Cameron on Monday!'

'Will we be in Sudan for Christmas?'

'Can we visit Ethiopia, too?'

Monday 19 May

Last Friday's homecoming was a 'high peak of happiness'. If only it could have lasted. Troughs of despair follow days of hopefulness. Today's trough has been more tedious than most. Now, when I expected steady recovery after the reassuring medical report, I'm stuck with increasing disability. And Les has to watch, seeing it get more marked each day. To add to his own problems (no further word from Sudan) he has to do countless little things for me — shutting the car door, opening tins, fastening my buttons, getting me up and down stairs ... I can't understand why my hands and feet have become acutely painful, and swollen; nor why a fever has developed …

'O God, please *do* something. Please take it all away. I can't go on like this.'

Tuesday 20 May

This morning's post brought Mother's fortnightly letter. This time she shared an extract from a book, *Seeds of Contemplation*, which she bought recently in an old Suffolk church.

'… but when the time comes to enter the darkness … in which we see the insufficiency of our greatest strength and the hollowness of our strongest virtues … then we find out whether or not we live by faith. It is in this darkness that we find true liberty. It is in this abandonment that we are made strong. This is the night which empties us and makes us pure.'

Those lines have been strangely comforting to me today, reminding me again that God's power is strongest when I'm weak. It will be lovely to see Mother next Thursday. She's coming up on the night train, arriving in time for breakfast. I hope I'm more mobile by then!

Thursday 29 May

We're all enjoying Mother's visit! I shall hate to see her go tomorrow. We've been out most days. This morning we went to Collieston. I'd always wanted to visit this quiet fishing village, nestling into the cliffs just north of the Ythan estuary. It's a delight! How I wish the youngsters could have been there. They'd have loved the small boats pulled up on the smooth yellow sand. We passed a spreading bank of sweet-smelling mint along the cliff path. All from one small root tipped out with the garbage? Bluebells and pinkbells were growing wild in the tall grass, gulls crying overhead … a sad, insistent sound.

And I actually *walked* along the rough cliff path! An exciting sense of freedom has come with this week's increasing mobility. Yes, I really am moving at last. Each day brings some new achievement. How glad I am for Mother and Les to see it!

'I won't need to unscrew the peanut butter jar for you much longer!' Stuart chuckled at tea-time.

'And you'll be able to drive us to the swimming-pool on Saturday, won't you, Mum?' said Rachel.

'Oh yes, easily!'

Anne phoned. 'How are things?'

'Guess what, I'm getting better all the time!'

'Oh *good*, that's great!' There was a pause, then: 'Pete and I have been praying that God would heal you. Is that what's happening?'

'Well, I haven't had any medical treatment, and all the tests have given normal results, so I guess it could well be!'

What a debt we owe to those who've cared and prayed over past weeks. And if this healing has been given in direct answer, well, I'm thrilled! Praise be! It's a humbling experience to fall so completely into the hands of God. I prayed so desperately for relief just ten days ago. Was that the beginning, the point at which I gave the whole problem to God and began to expect an answer? Not that the answer would necessarily be healing. God has the last word, and I am glad that it is so.

But if God has such power, why did he let it all happen in the first place? That seemed a reasonable enough question, until I remembered Mary Craig's comment: 'The human heart is very often (as arid) as a desert, but sorrow irrigates the desert.'

I'm beginning to take that in. Either I open myself to what sorrow can do — and grow — or my heart becomes more arid still. One way I have grown is in new understanding. I think I can understand the struggles of others a little more now. I'm beginning to feel *with* Les as well as for him.

Month 5

Sunday 15 June

Sunshine after rain. A beautiful Sunday — and the twins' thirteenth birthday! We set off to walk up Benachie together, the youngsters soon striding on ahead. We could hear their excited calls in the distance as we sat on a half-way seat overlooking the magnificent Aberdeenshire view — fields and woods and small lochs all spread out for our pleasure. How God delights to delight us!

I took particular pride in getting so far up the mountain. Four weeks ago I could hardly walk and now I was tackling Benachie. I can cycle again as well, and drive, write with ease, carry shopping ... Independence has never seemed so sweet.

There was a lot to talk about as we sat there. Yesterday brought another phone call from the company in Sudan. They want Les to fly out to Khartoum on Tuesday for interviews. The youngsters have been full of it:

'Lucky Dad, getting a free trip to Africa!'

'Will he fly a plane when he gets there?'

'Do they have a nice uniform?'

Les hadn't said much.

'How do you feel about this Sudan possibility?' I asked him now.

'Hopeful. But it's going to be hard.'

'If they offer you a job will you take it?'

'Yes, I think so. There's no choice.'

The youngsters came striding back down the peaty path.

'Hey, what are you doing sitting here? We've been almost to the top and back!'

It was time to go home to that birthday tea. The three of them raced ahead. Down amongst cool fragrant pines, I turned to Les.

'One last thing.'

'Yes?'

'Don't agree to any offer out there unless you're *sure* it's right, will you?'

'No. You know I wouldn't.'

Friday 20 June

This morning I retraced our path up Benachie — alone. Les left as planned. The wooden seat was already warmed for me by the sun. Larches were thrusting out new green fingertips; golden broom scented the air. Bees buzzed above the tufts of heather. A Forestry Department worker called a greeting as he strode up the steep mountain track.

Then all was quiet again, except for the sound of the breeze stirring the trees. Below me lay a kaleidoscope of greens. There won't be much greenery where Les is. What's the temperature and humidity there in June, I wonder? It's his third day — he should already have some idea about the future. So much depends upon this trip. I wish I were there, so that we could talk things over together.

My thoughts went back over the past three months. I'm glad they're over. We'll soon be out of this bad patch of unemployment! He must find a job by the end of the month. The final pay cheque's due next week. My illness has showed that suffering only begins to become bearable when it's turned to some creative point. Could that happen with Les's situation too? It seems impossible. But why else has God allowed this long series of setbacks?

At midday the sky darkened and large drops of rain began to fall. I took shelter under a small pine

as hail stones danced everywhere, and little streams
began to hurry down the dry pathway. Hadn't
reckoned on this! The storm slowly eased off, moving
out across the valley. I was soaked, but glad of this
away-day, even so. The break from routine is
important. It's good to step back and get a new angle
on things, even if the answers to some questions are
not yet clear.

Sunday 22 June

Made an unwelcome discovery this morning — a first
grey hair. I removed it in disgust!

The phone rang at tea-time. It was Les! He'd be
arriving at Aberdeen on this evening's flight. I
wondered why he was coming back earlier than
planned. I hadn't expected him till the middle of the
week.

Another 9 p.m. trip to the airport; another
meeting at the barrier, questions poised. Les looked
tired, tanned, dusty.

'I must shake that Khartoum sand out of my
shoes!' he said, before getting into the car.

'Any success?'

'No, I've turned down the offer.'

There was a pause as I tried to take it in. 'Why?'

'Well, it's a long story. But I knew it wasn't for
me as soon as I got there. Felt uneasy. And I'd never
have been able to stick it out alone, living in a hotel
for weeks on end. Being on the spot convinced me
that this job wasn't on.'

'But what about the flying? Did you do any?' Les
is desperate to be airborne again.

'No. When they suggested a check ride I didn't
accept, because by then I'd already made up my
mind not to join the company. It wouldn't have been
fair to go up just for the thrill of it. Would have cost
a lot, and their fuel stocks are low.'

It was still twilight as we arrived home —
midsummer now! The night air was scented with
wild flowers. Les slowly carried his gear indoors. My
feelings were divided — relief that he would not have

to leave us; fear about the uncertain future. What now? Who'd have thought it could prove so hard to find work.

Stuart called out. I'd hoped he'd be asleep. 'Hey, Dad, when do you start your new job?'

'I won't be taking it, lad.'

'Why?'

'Well, it just wouldn't have been right for me.'

'Oh, that *is* a pity. I wanted to go to Khartoum this summer!'

Monday 23 June

The last pay cheque has come. I'm beginning to watch spending at home. I haven't been too concerned till now, imagining that the work problem would have been solved by this time. It's not too difficult to save on food. I won't buy the monthly joint in future. We can do without butter, fancy cereals, most frozen goods. I'm glad the youngsters don't go much on things like cream or pork chops. Chocolate can be saved for a Sunday treat, and shop cakes bought now and then 'for special'.

'Anything else we can cut down on?' I asked Les.

'Well, we'll need to watch our use of the car — keep outings to a minimum. There's the phone, too. I guess we ought to think twice before we make a call.' He just looked at me — and I got the point.

I'm glad it's summer, so that fuel costs are lower. Electricity and telephone bills are due within the month. Rent, too. At least this is nominal, being a council house. What else? Oh yes, car tax and insurance coming up. No need to budget for the MOT, though. Our old Ford got through with amazing ease last month. A great relief!

Nothing further on the job side. Les spent most of the morning carefully scanning his 'world airline directory', marking off companies which use crews with his experience. This afternoon he got out the typewriter and started writing round. An airline in the Far East has replied to Les's recent enquiry with a duplicated letter: they'd consider an interview if

he'd pay his way out there and back. We really
laughed over that one!

There's a lot to do around the house, getting
things shipshape before the school term ends. I hope
to get a look-in on the typewriter later. Nine chapters
of the book are complete — just one to go. I want to
have it finished by 4 July when school holidays
begin.

Monday 30 June
Jack called in this afternoon while Les was off
helping to make a new path at the church hall.

'Tell him to come round some time. I've got an
idea!'

Les walked over to their house later. It was
nearly 9 when he got back. The usual verbal battle
was going on between me and the youngsters over
the issue of bedtime.

'Time's up. Away you go!'

'Just five minutes more, Mum. I've got to glue
this tail section on my bomber,' Murray insisted.

Stuart saw Les coming in. 'Hallo Dad, where've
you been?'

'The Mac's house.'

'Why?'

'They asked me to go.'

'Why?'

The youngsters are getting very inquisitive about
Les's movements. It's an indication of their own
bewildered, unsettled feelings. They wonder if we're
keeping facts from them. Les sank down on the settee
while I chased the lads off upstairs. Rachel edged up
close beside her dad. She seems to spend more and
more time doing this now, sometimes sitting right on
top of him! Perhaps it's her way of saying, 'You
won't leave us, will you? I'm going to keep you
anchored here!'

Much later, when we'd said impatient
'goodnights' to all three, Les looked up from his book.
'Jack has offered me a job with his company.'

'Wow, that's *great*!' (What a surprise!)

'It'll be a bit of an adjustment.'

'Why, what's it going to involve?'

'Assisting in the diving-equipment workshop. I'll be a spare pair of hands around the place. They're very busy at present and need temporary help.

'What hours will you work? How long will it go on for?'

'It's a regular 8.30 to 5.30 shift and I'll be paid by the week for as long as they need me. Maybe one month, maybe six months. We'll just have to wait and see. The pay's £25 per day, which is pretty good for an untrained worker!'

'When do you start?'

'Tomorrow. I'll take the car at first, but I may be able to share transport with Jack later on.'

'So it's all fixed up! You'll be back to an early start in the mornings!' I said, happily.

It's good of Jack to have arranged this! He knows from experience how devastating unemployment can be. And it's a big relief that Les has work to do, even if it is so different from flying a plane. It will certainly ease financial pressures.

I packed Les a sandwich lunch for tomorrow, while he looked out older clothes. It's odd for him to be wearing worn shirts and patched-up trousers for work.

Month 6

Tuesday 1 July

'July at last. Only three more days to go!' Rachel said, between quick mouthfuls of breakfast corn-flakes. 'Can't wait for school to end. It's even more of a drag this last week. Do we have to go, Mum?'

'Yes.'

'If only I could be like you and Dad, sitting around having fun at home all day!' Murray moaned.

'We don't just have fun, and Dad's working today anyway!' I told them. 'In fact he left early, just after Stuart.'

'What? Why didn't you tell us?'

'Where? What's he doing?'

The two of them gazed at me across the table, all agog. I gave them the details.

'Oh, not flying then,' said Murray, frowning in disappointment.

'Never mind, it _is_ work,' Rachel reminded him.

I hustled them off. The school bus would be leaving soon. They'd have to sprint up the road.

The day seemed odd. The house strangely empty and silent. I had lunch on a tray on the garden seat — the sun was trying to shine, air warm, strawberries faintly pink. Time to work on that last chapter. My mind turned to Wendy. Our own struggles seem small beside my sister's. (Her husband had only just managed to get work, after two years of acute arthritic disablement when their middle child — Simon, aged thirteen — was found to have a rare type of leukaemia, difficult to treat.) I can feel with her more now. Suppose it was our middle child — Stuart. How could I bear to watch him go through such suffering — blood transfusions, bone-marrow tests, lumbar punctures, nausea, bleeding, pain? I'd yearn to take it all away from him, but wouldn't be able to. I was back with that same recurring question. Could I endure it? Only, perhaps, by resting on God's faithfulness. But what about that? Doesn't suffering bring it into question, cancel it out? No, not unless I'm going to believe that God caused suffering. But he didn't; it results from sin and a world gone wrong.

God is there, still a refuge, still completely available to us — to Wendy — even in the worst possible moment. He understands. In Jesus, God himself suffered more than any man ever will. We can still trust God. This has been my refuge all along.

The youngsters were eagerly waiting for Dad's return this evening. He hardly had time to get the front door open before their bombardment: 'Did you like it, Dad?' 'What did you do?' 'Was it horrible being new?' 'Where did you get those overalls and funny cloth gloves?'

Over supper he gave details. 'Well, it wasn't too bad. Just a bit strange. I helped a man pull apart a high-pressure water pump and then we cleaned all the different pieces.' His section of the workshop services air-pressure-reducing valves for deep-sea diving-equipment, used in the North Sea oilfields. It sounded new and fascinating to the youngsters. Murray decided it was not such a bad change from flying, after all.

'Just a bit strange.' What an understatement. Workshop labouring must seem *very* strange, just four months after leaving the flight-deck of a passenger aircraft. 'It's only temporary; he'll soon be back on some other flight deck', I keep reminding myself. And he's grateful he's now able to provide for family needs. It restores his self-respect. That fact is helping Les to accept this job. The workshop is thirteen miles away, right beside Dyce Airport. That's tough; he must be constantly aware of planes coming and going close by.

Friday 4 July

Les is getting into the work routine. Jack picked him up this morning in his company car. That's another big help. Our Ford's greedy on petrol.

I couldn't wait to get that book finished. Would I make it by 4.30? I spent most of the day tidying up and typing the last chapter. By 4 p.m. it was nearly done. The last sentence and covering letter were completed at 4.25.

At 4.30 the children rushed in through the back door — the school holidays have begun!

Everyone was buzzing with excitement over supper.

'What shall we do these next six weeks, Mum?'

'Can we go away somewhere nice? Everyone else is. Fiona's even flying to Turkey tonight!'

'Why not take a trip to Aviemore. That's a magic place!'

'You won't make us do maths homework *every* day, will you Dad?'

Les explained that we can't go away this time. The children understand this and they accepted it, though we sensed their deep inner disappointment.

'Let's plan some away-days,' I suggested quickly. 'We could each choose a Saturday outing for everyone to enjoy.'

They seemed to think that was a reasonable plan. Stuart claimed first turn.

'Can we go tomorrow, Dad?'

'Well, I suppose so.'

Les was tired. He's not used to spending long hours in a workshop.

'What did you do today?' I asked as we sat out on the back doorstep after supper.

'Cleaned a whole lot of valves, did a bit of painting, swept the floor, helped dismantle a diver's helmet. Kept pretty busy really.'

Stuart overheard this — he was just inside the kitchen, poring over an ordnance survey map and planning tomorrow's route.

'Dad, have you seen a diving-bell yet?'

'Yes, yesterday.'

'What are they like?'

'Small round things like a ball, about six feet across. Big enough for two divers and their equipment.'

'Can they see out as they're lowered down from the ship?'

'Yes, there are windows. The whole thing is well-insulated, of course, and coated with a thick layer of foam on the outside.'

'What does a pressure chamber look like?'

'They're long and round like a cylinder, and they stay put on the ship or oil platform. Divers live in them when they are not working on the seabed.'

'How big's a chamber?'

'Oh, about eighteen feet long, and six feet across, I guess. Just enough room for the same two divers. They transfer to the chamber when the bell's lifted back up from the sea.'

'How long would they stay there?'

'Oh, I don't know. Maybe two weeks or more. It must be horribly cramped.'

Stuart turned to his map again. I had a feeling that a trip around the northern fishing villages was in the offing.

'Better water those seedling carrots,' Les said. He's terribly proud of his success with them! 'Amazing how dry the soil gets down here by the river. Must be all the sand.' He picked a juicy just-ripe strawberry in passing.

Stuart gave me my marching orders. 'Please can we have a picnic lunch and tea tomorrow?'

Before bedtime Les looked back through this week's correspondence. The post hasn't brought much. Local Dyce companies are still not recruiting (Les keeps in close touch) and others in Britain usually answer, 'Thank you for your interest in the company. Regret that we cannot offer a position at present. Will keep your application on file.' Les is learning that a short letter always means a 'no' and hardly needs reading. He's still awaiting replies from a couple of foreign companies, one operating out of a Caribbean island. It sounds idyllic; a complete contrast to Sudan.

Saturday 5 July

We set off on Stuart's trip at 11 a.m., driving across rolling green farmlands towards Gamrie Bay and Gardenstown. I couldn't understand why so many other cars were heading down the same narrow cliff road. Then I saw crowds of people on the small quayside. Some sort of 'gala' was taking place. The local 'public conveniences' were being used as a platform from which announcements were made through a loud hailer.

Two teams of fishermen lined up for a tug-o-war across the narrow harbour outlet. Cheers of delight! The whistle shrilled and the tug began. Grunts and groans were drowned by loud shouts of support. The teams were well balanced; the taut fisherman's rope hardly shifted. Then a sudden jerk, and the men on the near side hauled back a foot or two. There was an excited roar from the crowd. The team on the far side mustered strength and gave a huge, determined tug. Their opponents tottered on the very edge of the harbour wall, then fell headlong down into the chilly water, rope and all. There were shrieks of laughter, clapping, 'Weel done, lads!' from the hailer. It was all part of the gala fun!

We parked the car in a narrow street of fisherman's cottages and walked down to the pebbly beach. Nets were draped like giant spider's webs across drying-posts. It was quiet there, all the activity centred on the harbour. The tide was out and gulls preened on the rough shell-covered rocks. A narrow path led us up some steps and round the headland to Crovie. There was tideline litter everywhere — a disgusting, unexpected sight along so lovely and lonely a stretch.

Crovie came into sight now. Just a thin line of fishermen's homes nestled into a sweep of the cliff. They're used mostly for tourists in summer. We passed holidaymakers moving their gear from the car park to a rented cottage at the far end of the row. It was all being done by wheelbarrow. There's a small shop in Crovie, and a gem-cutter's display. We passed the jetty, and dodged washing on a beach-side line. Les prised a sea-snail from a rock and we watched its thick brown sucker-pad grope outwards in sudden alarm.

'Don't forget we're going to Pennan too!' Stuart reminded us. There was just time to walk back to the car and set off along the narrow cliff-top lanes before dark clouds rolled up to spatter us with rain.

'I hope it's dry at Pennan,' Stuart said. 'I *must* launch my tug boat on its maiden voyage.' (Why didn't he do that at Crovie?)

The road down to the little village was very steep.

'Will the car get back up again?' Murray asked.

'Hope so!' said Les. 'Else we'll be here for the night.'

'Great!' (That was Stuart!)

The rain hadn't yet reached Pennan. The tide was edging its way in. Stuart selected a sheltered inlet. 'Just right for the launching!' he called out, hoping we were all watching. We sat in a row along the low harbour wall enjoying the sight of him slipping from one weedy rock to the next, while the small vessel chugged out towards the open sea. He'd forgotten to set the rudder in the right direction! Rachel and Murray hurried to help with recovery operations, falling into a couple of rock-pools en route. At last we settled down in the car for a picnic tea — 'Nice ginger cake, Mum!' — while sudden rain danced noisily on the bonnet.

'I hope everyone liked my outing,' Stuart said as we set off into gathering sea mist. The car groaned slowly up the narrow road. The cracked exhaust pipe sounded noisier than ever.

'Yes, lad, we all did!' I reassured him.

There's nothing like a good, long day of fun!

Friday 11 July

The youngsters are getting into the holiday routine. The twins went off on their bikes to the scrapyard this morning — a ten-mile round trip. They love picking over the 'carcasses' of cars. I hoped they wouldn't haul home too much junk. Fishermen were busy out on the Don, counting on success to offset the cost of the permit. We've seen several salmon rising this past week.

A letter came from the Caribbean company with a spectacular stamp. I was dying to see the contents, but left it till Les got in. Rachel went off armed with her catalogues. It's a lean month, with customers away on holiday.

The boys returned with a windscreen-wiper motor. That's all, but they were delighted. Murray saw a man in waders out on the river, casting a line, so he got his own tackle and set off to try for trout, digging up a large worm from the garden en route. He was back home within the hour.

'Caught our supper?'

'Yes, sort of.'

He'd hooked a small 'un but then couldn't bear the expression of pain on its fishy face, so gently released the trout and let it go. He'll never make a fisherman!

Rachel came in, discouraged. 'How on earth am I going to buy those shorts I need? And sun-glasses, and a sun-top and a new anorak? My earnings only come to about £11 this month.'

It's hard on her. She sees her friends getting nice new clothes, then showing them off, winning compliments.

'Let's talk to Dad and work out a plan,' I suggested. 'You get some of the things and we'll see about the rest. How's that?'

She muttered some sort of answer — not too communicative these days.

Les came in last, late from work, dumping his grubby overall and shoes on the mat.

'Look Dad, we've got this motor. It's magic!'

'Dad, Mum says you're going to give me money for a new anorak and shorts!'

'It's Saturday tomorrow. Can we all go to Balmedie beach?'

Poor Les, swamped as usual. I pushed in with the letter. 'This came today!' He stopped to open it straight away, skimmed the too-brief contents and handed it to me.

'Well, that's that,' he said.

They've filled all the crew vacancies already.

Les was very tired again this evening, stretched out on the settee, eyes closed. Rachel spied his Friday pay-slip on the sideboard.

'Don't forget I need at least £12 this week, will you?' she reminded Les, mischievously prising open one of his eyelids. He grinned. 'Daughters!' The reminder was tossed off light-heartedly. Inside I know he'd love to be able to provide more fully for her.

'I'm getting to know one lad at work quite well,' he told me later. 'We meet in the lunch hour. He likes reading, so I said I'd give him one or two books about Christianity. He seemed interested. He often asks what it's all about. Makes a change from the usual meal-break chat!'

'Do the others know where you've come from and what you were doing?'

'This chap does, but I haven't talked about it with the others. They're not interested, except for one fellow. He's keen on planes and likes getting information.'

Les gave today's copy of *Flight* a quick glance.

We get it every week now.

'Think I'll put something in under "Situations Wanted",' he said.

'That's an idea. Would they print it in the next issue?'

'They might. There's this regular "agency" advert here, too. I've been wondering whether to contact them. They could have something to offer.'

'It sounds like a good plan. If you write first thing tomorrow we'd catch the last post before the weekend.'

I was optimistic. Les wasn't so keen. He was too tired.

Saturday 12 July

Les posted the agency letter this morning. He'll phone in his 'Wanted' advert early Monday.

Alex and Kirsty invited us round for supper this evening — a real treat. I wore my new black skirt — made from the material I bought in Utrecht at Easter.

The meal was delicious. I never knew Kirsty was such an adventurous cook! I specially enjoyed her pumpkin pie. It was so good to relax, laugh and chat. We really unwound.

Sunday 13 July

Quite an out-and-about weekend. Tea at Lin and Trevor's cottage — the hedgerows in full summer dress. Queen Anne's lace spread out everywhere. Grain tall. Smart, flustered oyster-catchers still bustling around. Lin's welcome was warm. We sat in their newly-decorated living-room overlooking fields with pine woods beyond; cows russet-brown against the soft green. Trevor lit a log fire in the grate, flames paled by the sunlight.

'Are you really well again now?' Lin asked.

'Yes, it's marvellous to be free of all that.' I'd almost forgotten the whole episode. It seems ages ago.

The dog and cats joined us on a short walk through the shadowy woods. Then Lin invited us in to an enormous tea, laid out on the kitchen table. Just enough room for nine of us to sit down, but more than enough food — even for our ravenous lads.

Lin packed chocolate buns and fruit cake into a bag, then picked wallflowers and pansies from the garden.

'For you to take home!' she explained. I was touched by her kindness. It's one thing to give our family tea, another to send us home with gifts, too!

Wendy phoned this evening.

'Some days Simon's illness seems ghastly,' she said. 'Then someone calls in for a chat, or something small but unexpectedly helpful happens, and I'm suddenly reminded that it isn't all as awful as it seems. And that I'm not alone, either. God's still showing his care for us. I'm finding I *can* trust him.'

Simon has to go in for another blood transfusion next week. It's a relief to know that the series of lumbar punctures is over at last. He tries to go fishing with young Peter — both love it, Wendy says — but can't keep at it for long; he tires too quickly.

'Simon's awfully funny about that wig we bought him last week,' Wendy went on, 'He won't wear it, even though his own hair is so thin and straggly now. If I insist on taking it when we go out, he carries the thing round under one arm like some hairy animal!' She laughed as she told me. And I marvelled at her ability to find humour, even in this hard situation. It's quite an example, and it must ease the tension in their home.

Tuesday 29 July

Sandra came over this morning.

'Two bowls of strawberries for you!' she said. 'I've been out picking at a farm and brought home far too many.' They're huge, and more than make up for our own scanty crop. I was starting to pull off the stalks when the phone rang. It was Mrs P.

'Can I come over with some strawberries? Our garden's *full* of them and we can't possibly freeze so many.'

She drove round with two large, overflowing tubs. What a treat! I decided to make some jam. Murray cycled off to buy extra sugar.

'Umm, yummy smell!' Stuart beamed, peering into the bubbling jam pan.

'Any for supper, Mum?' asked Rachel.

'Just a few. Most are cooking.'

'Oh, that's a horrible waste. Fancy not keeping them for pudding.'

A car pulled up outside. It was Jane.

'Just thought you might be able to use a few strawberries from the garden. Mike's away and I can't possibly eat them all myself.' Three more bowlsful! I was almost speechless. What a day! So Rachel was able to have strawberries for dessert after all.

It's hard to know how to thank everyone for such thoughtfulness. I wish we could say our 'thank you' with some kind of repayment. But that would spoil their joy in giving. I must be content simply to accept in gratitude, without a sense of being in debt.

Les was amazed when he came in and saw our strawberry supper.

It was Rachel's turn to say 'grace' before we began. Thankfulness was something more than routine tonight, as I realized all that God *does* to prove his faithfulness. We've seen it in so many different ways recently– through the thoughtfulness of others, gifts, holiday times, outings, renewed health, Jack's provision of work, our beautiful surroundings ... the list is endless.

Later we walked over the bridge and along the narrow Fetternear road together. It gave us a chance to review job-application developments. Over the weeks Les has given me the gist of things, but I like details.

'The "Wanted" advert brought in one possible response, didn't it?'

'Yes, that group down south who're negotiating for a flying contract abroad.'

'Where?'

'Africa. No more details at present. They've told me to keep in touch by phone.'

'And the Agency just had that north Africa suggestion to make?'

'Yes, a year-long contract flying oil personnel. But it's still in the planning stage. No job-offers yet.'

It seems we've no choice but to go on waiting.

'If only something would happen!' Les frowned. 'I can't bear living with all this uncertainty.'

We walked on in silence. Sometimes there's no specific comfort to offer, only companionship.

'I've heard there'll be a number of crew layoffs soon in the UK,' Les said, as we turned back towards home. 'Several more pilots on the job-market already.'

'Why?'

'Oh, cutbacks. Part of the recession.'

'Surely it will only be temporary?'

'Not this time. Winter will bring crew redundancies after the busy summer flying, of course, but fewer men will be taken on again next spring.'

There was deep anxiety in his voice. I thought again of the factors which place Les in a less favourable position than most; the reason for leaving his previous company, his age (forty-seven), the steadily increasing time away from flying. Will he ever get back? Is there any point in hoping, trying, writing letter after letter, making call after call? Waiting for someone, somewhere, sometime to say 'yes'. Then Paul's words came back to me — 'I feel it's very important for Les to get another job *in aviation*.' We must go on — it's no good giving up now. 'I'd never get a comparable job in anything else anyway,' Les has told me. Nor would re-training seem to be much of a possibility at his age. In fact there's talk of cutting out such government courses — part of the recession.

A turbo-prop flew low overhead, approaching Dyce. I saw Les glance up. 'Last flight in from England,' he commented. It was the plane he used to fly.

Month 7

Friday 1 August

Murray's choice of outing this week. Tomorrow we go to Dunottar Castle. There was some citric acid left over from jam-making, so I decided to brew some special lemonade for the picnic. Rachel cycled to the village shop for three lemons. They're expensive, but it's a treat. I carefully followed instructions before leaving the whole panful on the draining board to cool. It smelt good. Extra vitamins, too.

Les got in late as usual on a Friday. He's not so tired now he's adjusting to workshop hours. Helping to wash the greasy supper dishes, he tipped the whole large saucepanful of lemonade down the drain. I spun round just in time to see the last dregs trickling away. I wanted to shriek out my dismay. All that sugar and expensive lemon juice gone. Citric acid, too, specially bought when I last went to Aberdeen. The angry words almost burst out. I snapped my mouth tight shut just in time. No good letting rip. Les wasn't to know. He thought that large pan was soaking.

'You've just tipped away all our lemonade drink for tomorrow!' I told him, still struggling to hold back my indignation.

'What? It looked just like water to me. Are you sure?'

Rachel giggled. I forced a smile. It reminded me

of two stickers the children put on our bedroom
mirror once, when Les was in bed with flu. One read,
'If your face wants to smile, let it', the other, 'If it
doesn't, make it'.

'I can go up and get you some of that nice
strawberry cordial instead, Mum!' Stuart offered.
'The corner shop will still be open.'

Saturday 2 August

Brilliant sunshine this morning! We drove across
country to Dunottar Castle, stopping on the way for
Rachel to take photos of a huge field of red and pink
roses (a rose nursery on Deeside). I've never seen
anything like it! We parked the car on the cliff-top,
then made for the castle — impressive as ever,
though the thick walls and high towers make me
shiver. It seemed sinister and hostile as we
approached up the stone steps. Gulls wheeled and
cried overhead, each sound echoing through the cold,
damp corridors of the shadowy ruin. Through a
window slit I could see an oil rig supply ship easing
by, and fishing boats marking a path across the still
waters of the bay.

'Let's go down to the beach for our picnic!' Rachel
suggested, and we were soon spreading ourselves out
along a driftwood log.

The lads couldn't wait to explore a nearby cave.
It was rather cramped and smelly inside. They
brought back a wet stone, red and veined. 'Looks just
like a lump of liver!' Stuart said.

Murray saw a small gull lying at the water's
edge. He approached slowly, but the bird didn't move.
He reached out and picked it up. 'Look what I've got!'
Frightened but unresisting, the young gull allowed us
to stroke and examine its sleek grey feathers. No sign
of injury, but it was obviously suffering. Kept
flopping on to a patch of coarse grass, head
drooping, eyes shut.

'May we take it home?' Murray asked. 'I could
keep it in a box in my bedroom.'

Les shook his head. 'No lad, it's going to die

soon, I'm afraid. Better to leave the gull in a
sheltered place beside the incoming tide.'

It was time to make for home. The sea mist was
creeping in, weaving its eerie way between ruined
castle walls. Les and Murray set off along the beach
and I saw the sadness on Murray's face as they
went. He hated to leave the kittiwake (Stuart
identified it) and carried the bird close against his
warm jumper. They set it down on the sand close to
the cave.

'Whose outing choice next?' asked Stuart on the
way home.

'Mine. To Aviemore!' Rachel informed everyone.

'Hope the car will make it,' Les said,
remembering all those steep roads in the Cairngorms.

'Course it will!' Rachel insisted.

It's been good to get out and about in the car this
summer. It's offset the youngsters' disappointment at
not going away on holiday. School begins again in
just over two weeks. Time's flown!

'Only a fortnight till the children's term starts,' I
told Les casually, later this evening.

'Good!'

I paused, choosing the words for what I wanted
to say.

'There won't be so much to do at home then.
Shall I go out to work?'

A look of horror shot across Les's face. He's
always been dead against my getting a job.

'No. Never. That would be the very last straw!'

'I thought you'd say that, and I'm relieved too. I
just wanted you to know I'm willing, if it will help.'

'It wouldn't. Forget the whole idea.'

That's got that clear. I won't raise it again. I'm
glad he's so adamant — I'd hate to go off each day.
My place is here, even more so just now, with the
youngsters unsettled. Anyway, if I did get a job it
would only compound Les's sense of failure. I
couldn't bear that.

Month 8

Monday 1 September

I turned out cupboards today, sorting junk for the autumn jumble sales. Les was home at lunch-time, taking time off to catch up on job enquiries. Nothing further from the Agency, or on the possible African contract. He's been phoning each fortnight.

Snack lunch at 1 p.m., then time to kill before Les could start his calls.

'They won't be available till after 2,' he said as we sat down with mugs of coffee.

'Rachel's new desk looks good!' I told Les. 'I see you've made it with strong supports underneath, too.'

I thought of the other things he's made recently — a new bathroom shelf, the mould for Murray's latest fibreglass yacht hull, a stile over the back fence ... I want him to know each item is appreciated. He isn't useless. We value *him*, as well as the things he does for us. I tried to put my thoughts into words for Les, but the message didn't penetrate.

'Nothing's going to alter facts. I'm still a failure,' Les said slowly. 'It even haunts my dreams.'

There was a long silence. How could I help? How could I convince him that it's not true. If only I could make him see and accept it. In April Paul said Les's self-confidence would only be restored by getting back into flying again. But each month moves us further from that possibility. There must be another way.

Two o'clock came. Les made half a dozen calls. Nothing, not even from Dyce.

'Try again soon,' the Agency said.

'No developments,' the secretary of the group down south replied. 'Negotiations still going on.'

How much longer? Don't they realize we're getting desperate?

'Sometimes I get angry with God,' Les said to me later, as we sat sorting old books and magazines. 'Especially when I'm cleaning the workshop floor. What's he doing through all of this? What's he trying to show me?'

The same old question — and no real answer.

'Maybe we can't get more light on that till after it's all over,' I said, thinking out loud. 'Maybe God's working out some sort of purpose in it, even now, which we won't recognize till we look back.'

'I suppose so, but it would be nice to have a hint or two.'

Tuesday 2 September

Shopping day in Aberdeen. Wet. Pigeons bedraggled. Litter floating across dirty puddles. But the spires were still magnificent against the grey skies. I caught the bus home this afternoon. Ailie joined me at the next stop.

'How's Les getting on?'

'Not too bad. Still at the workshop, but hoping to find something in the flying line soon. How's things with both of you?'

'Oh, Neil's not doing well with this self-employment idea. Job's going steadily downhill. Not likely to improve either.'

I can't help feeling for them. That new project looked so promising at first.

'If only he'd do something, try different possibilities — another line,' Ailie went on. 'I keep telling him he's a failure.'

'Oh no, Ailie!' I wanted to object. 'Don't ever say that. Build his confidence; show him how much you appreciate all he's trying to do.'

But I kept quiet. I sensed she was too upset to welcome any such suggestion.

Monday 8 September

'Happy sixteenth birthday!' we all called out as Rachel appeared for breakfast.

I bought a creamy chocolate cake at the village bakery for tea, and a block of vanilla ice cream.

'Hope you'll enjoy the boots this winter!' Les said as we sat round the tea-table. We paid half the cost as our gift. They're really posh. Enough to make schoolfriends turn green with envy! The twins bought Rachel writing-paper and felt pens.

'I'll pay for you to go swimming at the pool on Saturday for part of your treat, too.' Stuart told her — in an unusually generous mood. 'By the way, when I got those felt pens I saw a geometry set — just what I'm needing for school. Can I buy it tomorrow, Mum?'

'Yes, how much?'

'Oh, that doesn't matter. I've got my own money.'

I started to object. After all, buying school equipment is Mum's responsibility. Then I stopped, realizing how much Stuart wants to feel he's helping out, easing Dad's load.

After the birthday meal we had our usual family prayer-time.

'Let's ask God to help Dad find flying work soon,' I suggested.

'I'm getting tired of asking,' Rachel said.

'Yes, why doesn't he do something?' added Stuart.

'We don't know' is all we could say. But something else occurred to me.

'You're all getting older now. Maybe you're needing to learn harder lessons, just as you do at school. It's not that God cares or loves us less — quite the opposite. Because he loves and cares so much, he wants us to grow. Sometimes our trust needs exercise.'

Monday 22 September

This is quite a month for celebrations. It was our wedding anniversary over the weekend. Les took me out for supper in Aberdeen this evening. I didn't feel we should go to such expense, but he insisted on it.

'There's always a place for lavishness.' Les said. 'It's important!'

I'm beginning to see what he means. It's so easy to get stingy when you have to economize.

We parked the car in a side-street. Out in the main shopping area we discovered an attractive old building with bow windows. Soft lamplight and timbered ceiling inside. Just right for the occasion. Then, by the doorway, I caught sight of the framed menu.

'We can't go in here,' I objected, pulling Les away. 'It's much too expensive!'

He just smiled and held open the door.

'We're going in! Never mind the price. It's our celebration.'

I don't think I'll forget that meal. Not just because the Chicken Maryland was so delicious, and the ice cream sundaes so huge, but also because it has given Les such pleasure to splash out. Me too!

'Not very long till our "Silver",' Les smiled. 'Then we'll really splurge!'

Month 9

Wednesday 1 October

Today I felt I needed to take stock. Instead of
pedalling to the shops I lingered along the river-
side path (it reaches the village eventually!) absorbing
the spread of autumn loveliness. Blustery winds forced
the clouds across a shining blue sky, and sunlight
gleamed on almost-golden leaves. It was sad to see the
summer slowly dying. Bluetits were busy nibbling wild
rosehips and a dipper flitted between midstream rocks.

Back home again I sat by the fire (plastic coals
in our all-electric house) and spent time reading,
thinking, praying — even singing a hymn or two.
The cat hates the noise — thinks I'm going crazy!

Paul phoned just after supper, eager to know how
Les's flying contacts are developing. 'No further
news.' Paul was surprised. He'd thought something
definite would have turned up by now. 'I'll sit and
think up some more ideas,' he said.

The phone rang again (one of those evenings!). It
was Wendy.

'Don't worry about my phone bill,' she told me,
as we enjoyed a good chat. Simon is getting on
slowly. He can't go back to school yet, so visiting
teachers will start home-coaching soon.

'He's just been given a lovely big illustrated Good
News Bible,' Wendy said, 'and we've begun reading it
together. Simon chose John's Gospel. We've come to

the bits about death and everlasting life and he
wants to discuss them, so we do. It's helping me a
lot.'

I'm amazed at her frankness. It's hard to talk
about big, painful issues with those you love — but
so important.

'If anything happens to Simon I'll look back and
value these times we've had together,' Wendy said.

It's getting darker now; a cold frost creeping in.
The oyster-catchers have returned to the coast. Les
was home late from the church meeting this evening.
Vandals stole his bike lights last week.

'The first of October,' I said. 'You must be into
your fourth month at the workshop now.'

'Yes, and no sign that they'll pay me off yet.'

The cat jumped on to my lap, fussing for late-
night milk.

'The income certainly is a big help,' I
commented, getting up to make the cocoa. 'And
having work must help each day to pass.'

Les didn't answer. He looked tired and drawn. I
watched him sitting there, staring at the red light
which flickers round and round inside the plastic fire-
coals.

'If there's one thing I'm finding extra hard these
days it's being a "nobody",' he said suddenly. 'It
comes so hard after you've been used to
responsibility.' His remark really hit me. Les is the
serving type. He wouldn't baulk at emptying waste
bins, cleaning up thick black grease. But this
situation is really hurting him.

'Knowing it's only a stop-gap helps me through
the hardest days.'

'So job-satisfaction *is* important.' I'd been
wondering about that, ever since I overheard
someone say, 'People ought to be grateful to have a
job at all'.

'It's vital on a long-term basis.'

'Why?'

'Well, so much of our waking life is spent at
work. Eight hours or more. If people are frustrated for

that length of time, day in day out, they'll end up
screaming. Or worse. And they can't unwind when
they get home either — they're too strung up. That's
when the whole family suffers.'

Les doesn't often get so steamed up. He must have
been giving that one a lot of thought.

As I went to bed, I noticed the first deep pink
bloom on our sitting-room azalea! Early this year,
cheering up our winter.

Friday 31 October
Another whole month has slipped away. The last
touch of summer has gone. Winter's cold grey
depression is stealing into my own thinking.
Depression has always been 'another person's
problem.' Now it stalks me. I can't bear to face the
bleak reality, yet fighting the facts increases
frustration.

The door bell rang at 10 a.m. It was Kirsty. We
chatted over a mid-morning fly-cup. But I couldn't
relax, even in *her* friendly company. I was too strung
up. Why? It's ridiculous. I've never been the nervy
type before. I usually love company! I hope Kirsty
didn't notice. We chatted on about village bonfire
night — a big firework display is planned. Then
somehow we got on to the subject of these council
houses. They are on the market now, if occupants
want to purchase.

'It sounds like a very good opportunity.' Kirsty
said.

'Yes, ours is being offered at just over £11,000,
lower than the valuer's price because we've been
resident for over three years.'

'Can't miss a bargain like that!'

'No. We should be able to go ahead soon.'
Purchase of the house is number one priority as soon
as Les gets permanent work.

At midday, Kirsty went off to make the family's
lunch. I felt strangely tense as I waved 'goodbye'. Why?

'O God, please sort me out. It's so stupid.' As I sat with my lunch on a tray by the fire a battle was going on in my mind. I'd never realized before how crucial a person's mind is.

'The mind is its own place,' Milton once said, 'and of itself can make a hell of heaven, a heaven of hell.'

I'm afraid I'm not going to be able to cope with ordinary everyday situations involving other people, even close friends like Kirsty. My confidence is being undermined. I won't be able to chat with ease in the street, or across a shop counter, or over a cup of coffee. Committee meetings, informal speaking engagements, stewarding at church ... how can I go on with them? I'm beginning to dread the thought of going out, even to the shops. Entertaining, which I've always loved, now fills me with apprehension days in advance. I want to run away from people, yet I want and need them. What an extraordinary contradiction. It doesn't make sense. It's irrational.

If only I could talk to someone. But what's the use? How could I expect them to understand? 'Don't be so foolish,' I tell myself. 'You've got God, so you're all right.' But deep inside I am unconvinced.

'O God, what's the answer? The tangle's getting worse.'

This afternoon I tried to work on another humorous piece for the newspaper column (deadline next week). It wouldn't come right. I watched the river — golden beech leaves floating downstream on its gentle current, and twigs, too, torn from tired trees by last night's gale. One got entangled in a clump of reeds, caught up while the rest flowed easily on. But the water still moved around and beneath it, on towards the open sea. The small branch stayed there for a long time, completely stuck. Then, as I watched, it was unexpectedly eased away on the current, freed to continue downstream, released by the persistent current. Such a simple incident, yet it set me thinking.

I'm like that branch. I'm tangled up and I can't free myself. But isn't God able and waiting to do it all? — from start to finish — for me? How can I work this out? 'Have faith!' people say. But what if I haven't? Trust isn't an automatic thing. So does even faith have to come from God? That must be it! I've never seen it so clearly before. I've always thought I had to work up faith before God could do anything. Now I'm more forcibly aware than ever before of my helplessness — and there's hope in that! For Les, too.

Month 10

Sunday 2 November
This morning I asked God to help me when I met
folk after church — help me to be relaxed and
natural. I'm simply reaching up to God now, as a
child might thrust his hand into a parent's capable
grasp, and asking for his help. Just asking helps to
ease the tension. It certainly *is* making a difference.
I'm getting disentangled.

It must be my subconscious reaction to the
unemployment situation which is causing me to be so
strangely awkward with people. Present circumstances
make our family different from most around here and
this has a spin-off effect on relationships, even though
I don't want it to.

Monday 3 November
'Don't forget to let me know by phone if anything
hopeful comes in today's post!' Les called, as he
hurried out of the door to work.

I'm not likely to forget! I wait for the postman
every morning now, uneasy if the letter-box hasn't
clicked by 10 a.m. If he gives us a miss it's a terrible
let-down. Today was all right though — the letters
thudded on to the mat at 8.30. Anything from that
Agency? Or the group down south? I slit open an
official envelope with a hopeful postmark. It was the
airline with which the Agency has been dealing.

Fantastic! — they want Les to go down *this week* and discuss possibilities about that North Africa contract! I couldn't wait to phone Les, so excited I could hardly dial the number. He was thrilled, too, though he didn't show it. He never does! He phoned the airline immediately to make plans, then called me back.

They wanted him to go down south tonight! So he came home after lunch to put the documents ready in his briefcase, etc. I'm *so* glad for Les! The whole family shared the excitement as we saw him off on the bus.

'It will be on turbo-props again, won't it, Mum?'

'How soon will Dad go to Africa — will he be there for Christmas?'

'Lucky Dad, getting a trip down to London while we've got a whole miserable week of school ahead.'

I felt like ringing round and telling everyone. I did phone Paul. He was almost as thrilled as we are; full of optimism, too. 'I'll let you know the result!' I told him.

I hope the long train journey goes well and that Les won't be too tired when he eventually gets to Essex. In all the excitement I'd forgotten the implications of this new job possibility.

'It would mean being away on a year-long contract,' Les had told me. The terms are good, though, and he should get back on quick trips about every three months. I might even manage a visit out there myself. Once the year's over, there'll probably be openings in flying back here. Sounds as if it could all work out quite well — though I hate the thought of Les having to leave us. We must just wait and see what happens!

Tuesday 4 November

The phone rang at 4.15. I'd been waiting all day for Les to call.

'I'm coming back on tomorrow's train. Due in early evening,' he said.

'How did it all go today?'

'Good possibilities of something developing. They'll be writing later this week. We can discuss it all when I get back!'

Rachel quizzed me as soon as I put the receiver down.

'What did Dad say? Has he got the job?'

'When's he going, Mum?'

They're all agog! But there's not much to tell them yet.

I'm glad I bought some chicken today. I'll make a pie ready for Les's return tomorrow. I've found I can buy several uncooked chicken bones for 40p. There's quite a lot of meat on each, and it comes off easily once the bones have been pressure-cooked. A useful pie filling. Simpler living offers some welcome surprises! Pre-packed 'breakfast rashers' have been another. The youngsters love them — minced bacon, shaped into rasher strips. No more wails of 'I don't like the fatty bits, Mum!' I probably wouldn't have discovered them if I hadn't started shopping around with more care.

Wednesday 5 November

A big welcome for Dad this evening!

'Come on, tell us all about it!' begged Stuart.

'Pooh, you smell of cigarette smoke from that train!' Rachel said, in mock disgust.

Murray stood back, watching us all with a quiet smile.

Les told them all he knows, then produced a big box of liquorice allsorts for us to share. I had an odd feeling he'd got more to say — and it came when the youngsters were in bed.

'I heard some unfortunate news today, just before coming back,' Les began.

'Yes?'

'Another company down south have just paid off several pilots, all qualified to fly the very plane being used for this North Africa contract.'

'Does that mean they'll take those crews in preference to you?'

'Yes, I'm afraid so. I'm OK on turbo-props of course, but would need to get the particular aircraft they're using type-rated on my licence. That means quite a lot of time and expense for the company. I've a feeling they're not going to be so interested in me after today.'

There was a long silence. I did not want to accept this possibility. It threatened to crush all my eager hopes for Les. This is the only flying prospect at present. The other company down south have given a final 'no'.

Paul phoned, eager for news. The latest development came as a shock and flattened his usual enthusiasm. It was hard for him to know what to say.

'We'll just have to wait on that letter still,' Les said later.

He laid out his greasy overall and boots ready for the workshop again tomorrow.

Friday 7 November

The airline's letter arrived this morning. I opened it, then phoned the news to Les. 'North African contract needs can all now be met by pilots with necessary type-rating,' it read. Les's application is therefore unsuccessful.

'That's the way the cookie crumbles!' Les said, hiding his bitter disappointment.

I just didn't know how to answer.

I cycled to the village, a strong, cold wind against me. Ailie was in the post office queue.

'How's things?' we both asked at once.

'Neil's doing much better!' Ailie smiled. 'Things seemed to slot into place all of a sudden, just when he was about to give up.'

'Oh, that's *good* news. I'm really glad for you both!' Their success encouraged me.

'What a relief for them!' Les smiled when I told him later. 'Now *we* need something to slot into place, too.'

The trouble is, we don't know where to look now. Everything at Dyce, in the UK, and abroad has drawn a complete blank.

'I still wonder sometimes if I should look outside aviation,' Les said. 'But I just don't feel right about it. The prospects are remote, too. Let's face it, no one's going to get excited about a 47-year-old ex-pilot with one O-level, who's also been a postman, milkman, taxi driver, and factory worker in his time.' He gave me a wry smile, then went back to today's crossword. We've started buying papers twice a week, but the 'Situations Vacant' columns are not too promising so far.

Tuesday 11 November

There's a frost most mornings now. The last lingering greens along the flower border lie limp and black. It's a dismal time of year, hope at a low ebb. What is there to look forward to? Spring is too far ahead to seem real. The school term (August to December in Scotland) drags on. It's dark when Les and Stuart leave home each morning; dark when they return. Only six hours of daylight. I don't think I'll ever get used to northern winters. Gloom seems to settle over everything, sapping strength and optimism.

The beech trees along the river-bank are cold and bare; skies almost empty. Only a few skeins of wild geese, passing over on the long southward flight. Old Nog is active in all weathers, though. His usual rock perch is now covered with autumn flood water. Three young cygnets are growing fast, feathers still grey.

'Are you well enough for work?' I asked Les before breakfast. He felt ill last night.

'Yes, I'll make it.'

At least it wasn't wet this morning, though chilly frost glittered on grass blades and a cobwebby rose bush. Les drove off in our car. Jack is away.

At midday I heard the familiar brake squeak. (We still haven't got it sorted!) Les had come home.

'I just couldn't keep going any longer,' he sighed, easing down into the armchair by the fire. He looked awful. I couldn't persuade him to eat anything, so I nibbled his lunch-box sandwiches instead.

'Must have flu,' Les said. But he refused to go up to bed. By mid-afternoon he was feeling worse.

'It's ages since I felt as bad as this. What do you think it is?'

'I'm not sure. Maybe the doctor could help?' I hardly dared suggest it; Les never seeks help unless he's desperate.

There was a long pause, then, 'Yes, maybe he could. Would I get an appointment now?'

I was surprised — he must have been feeling bad. I phoned the surgery. Yes, our doctor could see him in half an hour. Village life has definite advantages!

The doctor prescribed antibiotics — and 'no work for at least a week.'

'I can't possibly afford to stay off that long,' Les sighed when he got home. 'Temporary employees only get paid for days actually spent *at work*.'

I hadn't thought of that.

Thursday 13 November

Whatever did they do before antibiotics?

'I'm beginning to feel better.' Les said last night. This morning he was almost back to normal! In just two days. Amazing!

'I must start work again!' Les decided when we'd cleared away the sticky porridge dishes. He went to morning surgery and got the doctor's permission. Then, as he was heading out of the door for work, the postman arrived.

'I'll just see what's come,' he said.

There was a small brown envelope postmarked 'Croydon'. A note inside read, 'Our church financial committee met last week and decided that part of this year's income should be sent directly to you. So we are happy to enclose a small cheque.'

Small? It was large, and came as a huge surprise. We looked at one another in amazement, not sure just what to say, hardly liking to accept. Then I suddenly remembered something.

'Look, they've made the cheque out to the exact amount you'd have earned if you hadn't been off sick. Right down to the last pound!'

We were dumbfounded! And to think we'd hardly heard from those friends since leaving Ethiopia six years ago. God had given us concrete evidence of his care. He had arranged this provision even before Les got ill. This gift has given us both a real boost.

The azalea is bursting with buds now. Quite a picture. It wins compliments from each visitor. And we've had quite a few visitors these past few days. Some called to ask after Les. I am finding it easier to relax with people now. My confidence is slowly returning. I still have a few awkward moments, but they are less frequent. Progress!

Friday 14 November

The unemployment figures for Scotland over the past month have just been released: 11.3 per cent of the total population is now jobless. 'Aberdeen remains a hopeful area,' they say. 'Black gold' is the attraction.

'Not that the oil industry is making much difference to local aviation at present,' Les commented this evening. 'With the long winter ahead, companies are laying off more and more crews.'

'But surely they'll take some back in the spring?'

'Yes, a few. But they'll be after men who've missed only a few months' flying. By the time they recruit I'll have been out of it a whole year.'

At least there's no talk of lay-offs at the workshop. We're grateful for this steady income, though the hard labouring work is telling on Les.

'We seem to be managing quite well on your £25 a day,' I commented this evening, scanning the week's housekeeping expenses.

'We do at the moment. But wait till the bills come in. This winter quarter's going to be really expensive on electricity.'

I'll try cutting down more on the food bills, so that we can set aside funds for the end-of-year demands. We can still economize on things like orange squash, cocoa, biscuits. And I'll start to buy one Christmas food item per week, so that housekeeping expenses won't suddenly shoot up next month. If I get dried fruit and nuts over the next fortnight, I can make the cake and pudding.

Saturday 15 November
We made a shopping trip to Inverurie this morning.

'I've been wondering ... ' Les said slowly, as we drove back, 'if I should reconsider the Sudan job. What do you think?'

I was caught completely by surprise. I hadn't a clue such an idea was in his mind. He'd obviously been giving it considerable thought. I knew I mustn't just leap in with objections, crushing all his tentative hopes. There was a long pause while I sat watching the tall straight firs of the forestry plantation slip by, rich deep green amid the drab November brown.

'I'm not at all sure. What was so clearly a "no" just four months ago can't suddenly have become a "yes".'

Les drove on in silence.

'I guess not,' he said, as we turned down our road. But I knew he was still thinking, wondering, hoping ...

It was fine enough to wash the car this afternoon.

'I phoned the company in Sudan from work yesterday,' Les told me. 'Their London office said the chief pilot's on leave in Britain.' He wiped the wet cloth gently over a large rusted area below the car door.

'So then I phoned him, too. Apparently there's another crew vacancy in Khartoum. He's going to look into it as soon as he gets back. He'll write and give me more details.'

'So there's quite a strong possibility of work there?'

'Seems so.' Les bent down to inspect the noisy exhaust pipe. 'I should be able to wire this weak bit up. It'll take care of the problem for the time being.' Then, 'I feel I must try the company in Khartoum again. They've been the only group to offer me work over all these long months.'

There was a hint of hope in his voice, so I kept my hesitations to myself.

It was quite dark by tea-time. I'm trying to concentrate on the bonuses of winter. One is that we spend more time doing 'family things'.

Tonight we read another chapter of *A Walk Across America* together. We're enjoying making this long journey in Peter Jenkins' company. Murray's specially taken with the dog, Cooper. It's a fascinating story — told so vividly that we're participants, instead of mere onlookers.

Sunday 16 November

There was a powdering of snow as we set off for the village kirk. But the small building was as warm as ever. The minister stood up to share today's sermon text.

'A rather unusual verse,' he began. 'The words of Jeremiah: "You shall *not* return to Egypt."'

I gave Les a quick nudge (the pew back is high, no one could see!). He was already smiling. We both realized that those six words have a special meaning for us, though the minister was quite unaware of the coincidence. Later, as we walked back over the hill towards home: 'I don't think I should consider Sudan further after that sermon!' Les smiled, giving me a wink. I knew he wasn't joking, though.

'Some people might laugh to hear you take Jeremiah so literally!' I said. But neither of us had any doubts.

We took a short cut across the crisp white grass. The village children were skating on a large frozen puddle. Marvellous fun!

'What will happen when that chief pilot contacts

you?' I asked.

'I don't know. I'll have to take it as it comes. I
can't help feeling that if God has given me such a
"no", he'll take care of the consequences.'

Les carried on home while I called on Anne to
collect some magazines she'd saved for us. Easy
Sunday reading. As she opened the back door there
was a delicious whiff of 'roast'. Anne's family were
already sitting round the table while Pete carved. I
hurried off, not wanting to interrupt.

And suddenly resentment hit me.

'Why can't *we* live like that now?'

'Why can't *we* enjoy a Sunday roast?'

'Are we being too hard on the children? Is it
fair?'

All my suppressed indignation surged up. I'd
tried to forget it, but it was there. There was
bitterness, too. Hadn't I every right to feel as I did?

'Why should we have to go on living like this?
Nine months is long enough. Surely we've learnt all
we need to know about humiliating circumstances?'
Something deep inside me wanted to shriek '*Stop!* I
won't live like this any longer!'

I was nearly home, dark clouds blowing across
from Benachie. There'd be more snow soon. The
house was warm and welcoming. Rachel was laying
the table for lunch. The curry smelt good.

'Scrummy!' smiled Stuart, seeing me put out nuts,
sliced banana, chutney, coconut. His one expressive
word of appreciation pulled me up sharp. He's not
feeling hard done by. None of them have ever said
'Why can't we have roast beef Mum?', or yearned for
any other delicious item of food. Why worry, then?

In the late afternoon, feet up by the fire, I
enjoyed Anne's magazines. I felt an occasional
twinge of guilt at my earlier outburst. Not that I was
entirely ready to give up my mood of self-pity. Then I
thought, Am I only willing to accept our present
circumstances if I can see some value in it?

Well? Who says the youngsters aren't getting
some good out of all this? Aren't they learning that

happiness doesn't just depend on fashion clothes,
and fried steaks, and Mediterranean holiday trips?
Surely hard circumstances are the soil from which
contentment grows?

The thoughts went round and round in my mind
— gradually 'coming from minus to plus'. I need so
much to share in other people's joys, to 'rejoice with
those who rejoice'. Yet it's hard. Resentment has to
go before it's possible.

Les gave Paul a ring, hoping for new ideas. Paul's
been putting out various feelers (good thing he's right
at the hub of things down there!) and suggested a
possibility in Cambridgeshire. Light aircraft flying —
similar type to those Les flew abroad. Les will make
further enquiries this week. *Flight* rarely features job
vacancies now. The companies would be inundated
with applicants if they advertised.

'I dread to think how many other pilots have
joined me on the job-chase recently.' Les said as he
put the phone down.

Another week at the workshop starts tomorrow.
How much longer will Les be there? Jack is due to
collect him as usual at 8 a.m. Our car has developed
a clutch-plate problem. I must remember to call in at
the village garage in the morning. Hope they can
repair it in the next few days.

Saturday 22 November
So good to have Father with us this weekend. I
packed a picnic lunch ready for a drive across to
Terpersie Castle and the Correen Hills. (The car's in
good form now.) The countryside was basking in
warm, unseasonal sunshine.

'There's the castle ruin!' Stuart announced, as we
approached up a narrow lane. It looked as forlorn as
ever. A sapling, growing up from the crumbling stone
floor, was its sole claim to life and hopefulness. We
tramped on along sheep trails, crossing the tumbling
burn before starting to climb the first hill-slope.
There was an old farm just ahead, surrounded by a

clump of gnarled yews. The youngsters were already
running from one stone-walled room to the next,
footsteps and voices echoing through the steading.
The roof had long since disappeared, inviting the
spread of grass and shrubbery to carpet the rough
floors. We ate our lunch in front of the kitchen hearth
and wondered how long it had been since the lady of
the house baked oatcakes and turned griddle
pancakes before the steady heat of a peat fire.

The youngsters raced us to the top of the first
hill. We gazed out over the spread of sunlit
countryside stretching away towards the Dee.
Magnificent!

'And to think this is almost the last weekend in
November!' I don't think Father's too keen to leave
on Monday. There have been floods down south.

This evening we reminisced about East Africa.
Father's still missing his medical work in Kenya.

'Remember those lush tea plantations? And miles
of white sand at Mombasa?'

'I wish I could suck the flesh out of a mango
again — or a paw-paw!'

'Remember all those "air safaris" around the
northern frontier?'

'Terrible place!' Les said with feeling. 'Hot, dirty,
thirsty country — stretching mile after mile after mile.
Sand everywhere. In your eyes, nose, mouth, clothes,
food, drinking-cup. I couldn't wait to get back to cool,
clean Nairobi again.'

'At least you could escape from it all after four or
five days.'

'Yes. No such prospect for all those Turkana
existing there, year after year. I still think of them
sometimes, constantly trekking from dry river-bed to
dry river-bed across that empty scrubland —
desperate for enough water to keep starvation at bay.
All that most of them owned was an old gourd or a
rusty tin, and the grubby goatskins they wore.'

It was hard to imagine such a hot, horrible place
on a chilly November night in scenic Scotland. Les's
vivid description suddenly hit home. The harsh

existence of the Turkana contrasted sharply with our ease and comfort here. We're living off the fat of the land by comparison. Our possessions fill this roomy home, and every basic need is met. I don't like to admit it, but my discontent and sympathy-seeking haven't a leg to stand on!

Friday 28 November

The first real blizzard of winter blew up this afternoon. An angry wind howled round the houses, flinging fat snowflakes against heavy doors. I'd be glad to welcome the family safely home. I hoped the roads weren't blocked. Snow ploughs and grit lorries may not be out till tomorrow. Rachel and Murray made it by 4.30, coats heavy with snow, eyebrows white.

'Good thing I've got my snorkel parka at last,' Murray muttered.

Les was in around 6. 'The roads are getting very bad, and the wind's terrible,' he said. Would Stuart's bus get through? He burst in at 6.20, tracking snow right through the house.

'I can't wait to get on top of that fire!' he cried. 'The heating wasn't working on that bus.'

'Good, pizza!' Murray beamed, as I served supper. At least the first course was piping hot. I didn't dare tell them we'd fruit salad to follow! The living-room was warm. Everyone was happy to be home for the weekend. I could forget the blizzard.

'I'm going sledging before breakfast!' Murray announced.

'If only we had skis,' said Stuart. 'How about a pair for Christmas, Dad?'

Rachel has to collect her catalogue order from the village shop tomorrow. The sledge will be useful for that, too. The snowfall's going to be fun once the wind has dropped.

Stuart turned to me. 'Something's stuck in my throat. It won't go down.'

'Get yourself some water then.' He brought a

glass back to the table and had a drink.

Seconds later he slumped forward across the table.

Les leapt up and tipped him back — chair and all. There was a sharp crack of breaking wood. Les bent over Stuart, trying to keep the airway clear. I knelt beside him, shaking with fear. I couldn't believe what was happening. Stuart seemed lifeless — vacant eyes wide, face and lips blue. Panic gripped me. What could I do? No time to call for expert help. We had to act immediately. Les was managing to keep Stuart's mouth open. I quickly reached a finger down into his throat. No apparent blockage. We tried to turn him over and slap his back. It made no difference — he still wasn't breathing. The heavy, empty silence was agonizing. We were losing our son. He was going. Nothing we could do made any difference. I bent down to try the 'kiss of life'. And in that moment Stuart suddenly gasped, then started to take in quick, shallow gulps of air. Pink flushed back into his cheeks. I was overwhelmed with relief!

Still kneeling on the floor, I cradled his head in my hands, trying to soothe and reassure him. The crisis could only have lasted seconds. It seemed like hours. Rachel and murray were pale with fright. They began to pick up the overturned coffee mugs, broken chair, Stuart's half-empty pudding dish. Then, still shaking, we all paused while Les prayed.

'Father, you've been so good to us … ' None of us will forget that moment of deep thankfulness. Stuart had been given back to us again.

What could have caused the problem? Did Stuart choke on a piece of apple? If so, had it now gone further down into his lungs?

'It could start up an infection. Perhaps I should phone and ask the doctor for advice?' I said to Les.

'Good idea.'

I emphasized that the crisis was over. I didn't want our doctor to venture out in this awful blizzard. Stuart was resting on the settee now, pale, but fairly bright. The doctor insisted on driving over straight away, though I tried to dissuade him.

'No, I need to see the lad,' he said. 'Doesn't sound like a straightforward choke.'

He brought his Land Rover — 'I can get through most weather in that!' Stuart was in bed by this time. After seeing him the doctor drew us aside.

'No need to worry about the piece of apple,' he said. 'But I am concerned about the episode. I'll check again tomorrow, then we'll decide what to do next. Don't worry. He seems to have got over it well!'

It's late now. Snowdrifts are still piling up outside. The cat is adamant: she will *not* go out before bed tonight. We can't even budge the back door! (It opens outwards.)

My mind keeps re-living that frightening scene. Will I ever forget Stuart's cyanosed face and limp body? We think we're so independent — yet our very breath is a gift from God.

Saturday 29 November
Stuart was in fine form this morning. He couldn't think what all the fuss was about. The snow is about fifteen inches deep: several drifts, too. Les forced the back door open and dug out the car.

'It looks like an igloo on four wheels!' laughed Murray as we climbed in.

It took quite a while to drive the short distance to the surgery.

'I'm very well, thank you!' Stuart told the doctor. He was afraid he wouldn't be allowed to sledge today.

'Good! You can do anything you like except climb trees, ride a bike, or swim without supervision,' the doctor said.

He will arrange for Stuart to be checked over by a hospital neurologist. We should be sent an appointment soon.

Month 11

Monday 1 December

The snow is starting to thaw. Stuart is in good form:
back to school today. Still no word from the chief
pilot in Sudan.

'Do you think you'll hear from the company
now?' I asked Les over our early mug of tea.

'No, they must have decided not to contact me
after all.' Rather surprising, after their assurance of
an early reply. Never mind. It will certainly save Les
some complicated explanations.

The garden's been damp and dripping in today's
warm sunshine. I suddenly caught sight of my
'winter flowers' along the back border. They're
coming into full bloom, despite the cruel weather. A
real surprise! The youngsters will be pleased (the
parent plant was their Mothering Sunday gift two-
and-a-half years ago). It's amazing how such delicate
primrose-like buds can shoot up and open out above
the crispy cold snow.

This afternoon I picked a small posy to take to
Jen. Life is extremely hard for her just now, with a
husband gone and two small children to care for
alone. I tried to feel *with* her as I pulled on my boots
and set off up the path to their house.

'Young Tim's got to go into hospital for tests
soon,' Jen told me, 'but I won't let them keep him
there over Christmas. It's going to be different for us

this year and I want to make the day as happy as possible for the kids.'

I can't help admiring Jen's strong, positive way of tackling tough circumstances. She must have her 'downs' but she always seems to bounce back. This impressed me today. The 'winter flowers' and Jen have given me a real boost.

The invoice for car repairs was waiting on the mat when I got back. A happy surprise — the bill's not nearly as big as Les feared. That'll cheer up his Monday.

'I can't imagine how they've managed to keep costs so low,' Les said later, checking the figures. 'But it all adds up.' He turned to the job situation.

'Another week begun and still no new ideas to work on.'

'Except Cambridgeshire?'

'I'm still waiting on that. They've acknowledged my enquiry. Should be sending further details soon.'

Les got his employment file out of the cupboard and scanned the contents.

'I might try giving Bob a ring,' he said. Bob's based at Gatwick, so he's a good contact.

Les sounded cheerful as he chatted with Bob — like the 'old days', when they flew together abroad. It was good to hear them joking. Bob can't know how low Les feels at times. He probably guesses, though. He'd no suggestions but promised to make enquiries. He'll phone back within the next few days. There's nothing more we can do.

Les sat down and challenged Murray to a chess battle. Stuart butted in with a complicated physics homework question. Rachel needed help sorting a muddle in her accounts. It all helps pass the time these long winter evenings.

The living-room smelt all spicy tonight. Christmas pudding on the boil. Cake about to come out of the oven. A good way to begin December. The youngsters are starting to count the days.

Wednesday 10 December
Big excitement: Les's birthday! I've been hiding a new badminton racket for the past fortnight. The youngsters put chocolates and new bits for his drill beside Dad's breakfast plate, saving the fun for later. We had a fish and chip supper, then chocolate cake and ice cream.

'I think I'll be twenty-one every day in future!' Les joked.

Murray frowned. 'If you were born in 1933, Dad, that makes you ... ' (He sometimes struggles with sums!)

' ... just a little over twenty-one?' Les suggested. The youngsters were in the mood for poking fun.

'If you don't get a flying job soon you'll be much too old,' Stuart said.

'He's getting a bit past it already,' Rachel butted in. '*We'll* find something better for you, Dad. Let's see, what can we suggest ... ?'

The three of them listed all kinds of way-out occupations, each trying to go one funnier than the last. (Their comments sounded blunt and tactless, but we understood. It is their way of trying to ease the inevitable tension.)

To add to the fun, I told them about my mistake at the supermarket last week.

'Guess what happened when Dad and I went shopping on Saturday?'

'Can't guess. You tell us.'

'Well, Dad pushed the trolley while I pulled things off the shelves. The place was packed and I was getting all flustered. I went on loading my arms with packets and tins till I could hardly see over the top. Then I dumped the whole lot into the trolley and made off in another direction. I was just ticking items off the long list when a tall, distinguished-looking man tapped me on the shoulder. "Excuse me, Madam, but you're loading up the wrong husband!" Did I blush! Then we both roared with laughter.'

'Good thing I was close by,' Les winked. 'You obviously need watching in those supermarkets!'

We've had a good day. Les is pleased with the racket. He'll be able to use it at the church hall court each week.

Friday 19 December

Christmas is just a long weekend away!

The youngsters couldn't wait to get home this afternoon. Last day of term! The Craigs have kindly lent us their portable TV. Rachel and the boys were almost beside themselves with delight. They've studied the *TV Times* from cover to cover, marking off favourites with big red circles. We couldn't get them away from the 'box' tonight. We had to put it in the boys' bedroom, so that Les and I could get a little peace.

Today's post brought a huge pile of cards and letters. The pinewood beams in the living-room are already festooned with cards — 120 at Rachel's last count. I'm quite overwhelmed by all these expressions of love and concern. (Most friends have had copies of the family newsletter we posted in July.)

'You're often in our thoughts,' they write across the bottom of a card. Or, 'Don't forget we're praying for you.' 'Please let us know of any way we can help.'

'We're certainly not alone in all of this!' I said to Les, smiling.

'I know,' he answered slowly. 'I just wish I wasn't the cause of such concern.' He feels so awkward about it — almost embarrassed. I hadn't been aware of this till now.

We heard Stuart's deep, booming laugh coming from the bedroom. There's a comedy film on.

'Any word from that neurologist yet?' asked Les.

'No, probably due to the Christmas postal rush. We should hear soon.'

'That reminds me,' Les said. 'I must try to mend that chair tomorrow!'

Monday 22 December

'Don't forget to bring home our Christmas tree, Dad!' called Rachel as Les set off for work this morning.

The front step glistened with frost. It was still dark outside (shortest day yesterday) but the sky was clear. I doubt if we'll have a white Christmas this time.

It seems hard for Les to have to go off to that workshop while the rest of us have such fun at home. He needs a break. He's very tired and suffering from a second boil. He'll take time off over Christmas though — enough for a long weekend.

'Only three days at work this week!' I reminded Les as we both scraped ice from the car windows. Jack's abroad on business at present, so no lifts to the workshop.

It took a while to get the car started (the battery's almost at the OAP stage!), but it groaned to life at last.

'Must rush!' called Les, pulling out from the kerb.

'Not on these icy roads!'

I needed to plan my day — lots of Christmas preparations to complete. Rachel was keen to spread royal icing on the cake. The lads could put out nuts and fruit on the coffee table. There was that big basket of goodies from Mary, too. And chocolates from the couple at '54'. (Aren't friends kind?)

Upstairs this afternoon I wrapped a few small gift items of my own. Mr. E. might like shortbread — it must be hard to housekeep when you're old and alone and housebound. Miss M. too — I mustn't forget her talc. I'd got a fancy candle somewhere that might just cheer up the Mathieson's Christmas table this year. (They've been through such a rough patch lately ...) It's good to be able to give, as well as receive — and so easy to neglect this when you need to economize at home. I mustn't get stingy.

A letter from Cambridgeshire arrived by the afternoon post. I hoped Les wouldn't be late home. Rachel heard the car door slam and rushed out.

'Where's the tree, Dad?'

'Sorry, I couldn't get it. The forestry shop had just closed when I got there.'

'Oh, that's really spoilt our evening. We've had

the decorations ready all day.'

Poor Les. Some homecoming. I handed him the letter. There was an application form inside, and a note suggesting he returned it as soon as possible. That looked hopeful!

'I'll fill it in this evening and post the lot off tomorrow,' Les said.

'How's the boil?' I asked.

'Oh, not so bad.'

'In a party mood?' It was the night for the church party.

'Sort of.'

He felt better for some aspirins and a new dressing. So we smartened up and set off. I had mixed feelings about being with so many people. That miserable shyness threatened again. But I seemed to hear God saying, 'Don't forget I'll be there too!' and that helped.

The party was fun, after all. I sat and chatted with the older folk most of the time. My heart sank when a 'forfeits' game was announced. I couldn't possibly sing a solo or demonstrate the Highland Fling! But, big relief, my name didn't get picked.

Tuesday 23 December

There was great excitement when Les walked in with the tree this evening. 'At last!' chorused the youngsters. It took them about ten minutes and a good deal of bickering to drape the branches with finery.

'Now Christmas is really beginning!' Rachel laughed. She and the lads have already hung the familiar decorations around the room — the star from Holland, streamers from Granny, angels from Woolworths. It looks so colourful! I've a feeling this is going to be a good Christmas, despite all.

Wednesday 24 December

Christmas Eve. A working day for Les, but we planned to welcome him home with a celebration supper. Rachel enjoyed rolling and folding another lot of flaky pastry. The house was filled with the delicious smell of sausage rolls and mince pies. Stuart was arranging chocolate wafer biscuits on a plate. Murray was finding room on the table for Rachel's cake.

The curtains were drawn across the frosty winter's evening. Candles threw dancing shadows against the pale ceiling. A carol was playing. Coloured lights blinked from the tree ...

Les walked in at 6 p.m.

'I've been paid off,' he said.

His temporary job had lasted since June. We had been grateful for it, even though labouring came hard after sitting at the controls of an airliner. Now it's over. Les won't have to get up early and go off to work over the holiday week. He'll be home to share the celebrations with us.

I could only think of this as I put plates of food on our candlelit supper-table. And I am still grateful.

It is Christmas Eve and the blow is somehow softened ...

Christmas Day

A quiet, happy celebration together. Today's gladness helped to ease the anxiety over Les's sudden redundancy. The youngsters giggled as they opened early morning stockings. I'd bought them a packet of table jelly each, and stuffed it into stocking-toes. (They're always yearning to nibble jellies from the larder shelf.) Aberdeenshire 'buttries' (rolls made from flaky yeast dough) for breakfast, then gift-giving around the tree. Rachel and Murray were pleased with the large drawing-pads and tubes of paints we'd chosen for them. Stuart had a new stamp-collector's file. Les was very happy with the 'Messiah' record I gave him. We both had the same idea this year — he's given me Faure's 'Requiem'. So we've some good listening ahead over the gloomy winter evenings!

A brief church service — lively carol singing! — then our roast chicken lunch with Christmas pudding to follow. It seemed to go down well. Coke and crackers added a special touch of excitement for the youngsters. We just had time to watch the Queen's broadcast before Miss M. arrived for tea. I'm glad she could come. I hated to think of her being alone all day in that tiny cottage. Not much room left for mince pies and fruit cake.

'Time to go to Monymusk!' Les announced at 6. We drove Miss M. home, then set off for the farm. It was thoughtful of the Blacks to include us in their programme. Most large families appreciate a chance to be by themselves for the Christmas festivities. Eleven of us celebrated together, enjoying traditional goodies, while real candles flickered on fragrant branches of a tree cut from the nearby forest.

Last thing, Les and I sat down and looked back over the day. Circumstances *haven't* spoiled our Christmas. It's been great!

Sunday 28 December
It's good to have Les home with us this holiday-time! A long lie-in each morning. And his boils have healed at last.

But I can sense Les's increasing anxiety. There's little opportunity to talk, now that the youngsters are home. I can imagine the thoughts churning round and round in his mind. 'What now? Where shall I look?' 'I *must* get an income from somewhere straight away.' 'I should be able to get temporary work until the Cambridgeshire job materializes, or another opening.' 'I'll buy the local paper tomorrow; start phoning round.'

The youngsters watched TV in the bedroom this evening. Les stretched out in the fireside chair, cat on lap, deep in thought.

'I'm trying to compose an advert for the "Situations Wanted" column of the local paper,' he said. 'Can you help?'

I fetched a pencil and we worded it together:
'Airline pilot seeks work for 3
months or more, or more, or more.
Anything considered.'
That should intrigue them!

Stuart came in and sat down sideways in the other
armchair. He's getting huge! Hefty too.

'When am I going to be able to ride the bike
again, Mum?'

'Soon, I expect.'

'Tomorrow?'

'No. Why?'

'Murray and I are planning another scrap-yard
trip. I saw them towing in a super wreck last week. It
looked great! We must go and pick it over.'

'Well, I'm sure it can wait a week or two.'

'Oh, Mum. Please?'

'No. Sorry lad.'

'What about swimming, then? Won't you even let
me do that?'

How he hates these restrictions, specially when
he's feeling so well. I hope we hear from the
specialist soon.

Tuesday 30 December

Quick work on that advert. We found it in the
morning paper today — and waited for the phone
calls!

The letter-box flap clicked. Murray ran to pick up
the letters. Christmas cards are still coming in, too.
There was nothing from the hospital. 'But here's a
Cambridgeshire postmark!' I called out to Les.

He scanned the contents. 'They've had a deluge
of applicants,' he told me, 'even though the position
was never advertised. They'll be short-listing six
pilots within the next ten days, then letting me know
the outcome.'

'You're sure to be one of them, Dad!' Rachel
assured him.

'Not much chance,' Les answered. His usual

pessimism kept him from getting excited. It seems to spark off my optimism. I can't help feeling he *will* be picked!

I cycled up to the village shops. The larder shelves were rather empty after the long Christmas holiday. I overheard several excited voices making New Year plans. Hogmanay's the big thing up here. It still seems odd to me, even after four years.

Mrs B. waved me down on my way home.

'A friend handed me this envelope. Yours, isn't it?'

I looked at the name and the official hospital stamp.

'Yes. It must have been sent to the wrong address. Thanks for passing it on.'

Stuart's appointment! I hoped we hadn't missed it after the long delay in reaching us. No! It's for Monday 19 January. Still another three weeks to go.

'The phone's just rung!' Les told me, as soon as I walked in through the front door.

'Yes?'

'Someone about forty miles north of here, looking for a pilot to fly a private plane. Business trips to London mostly. There are other, non-flying aspects to the job, too.'

'Sounds quite interesting. Are you going to look into it further?'

'Yes, on Friday. I'll drive up there for an interview. The chap wants to see me at 11.'

There was a hopeful gleam in Les's eyes. It did me good to see it! He smiled as he said, 'Fancy getting an answer to that advert already!'

'Yes, and something in the flying line, too!'

Les went over to the bookcase and opened up a road map.

'Up in distillery country,' I heard him say. 'Beautiful area!'

Part Two
Hope Against Hope

Month 12

Thursday 1 January

1980 past and gone. A big relief. Who'd have thought
Les would *still* be out of flying work? Never mind, this
first day of 1981 has brought a surge of new hope.
We'll probably have something all fixed up before
January ends. I've realized today that with God hope
isn't a 'maybe' — his answer to our problem is a
certainty, even if it's different from what we've been
expecting. Sometimes my trust is at a low ebb. But
not today. There's happy anticipation in the air.

It snowed quite heavily last night. A white
Hogmanay. Bright sunlight this morning set
everything sparkling. I couldn't wait to get out and
revel in it all.

We set off for Parkhill around 12. It was good of
folk there to invite us to a special festive lunch. Fun
to trudge across an unspoiled field of smooth, crisp
snow.

'Like walking over the top of a wedding cake!' I
said to Les.

'How do you know?'

Lunch was delicious. Stuart couldn't resist a
second helping of roast beef. There were strawberries
and cream for dessert — Les's favourite! After the
meal there was time for laughter and frustration over
one of those impossible-to-solve puzzles. Matching up

coloured sides on six blocks looks simple — till you've been struggling for half an hour.

The snow slopes were crowded with local children as we slipped and slid home. The cold bright air was alive with excitement. Sledges, skis, and plastic tubs everywhere. 'Magic!' cried our lads, hurrying into the house to find old clothes and rubber gloves and join the snowball war!

Friday 2 January

I waved Les off just after breakfast, to be in good time for that 11 a.m. interview.

'Hope Dad gets the job!' Stuart said over lunch. 'He'd have a great time flying one of those smaller twin-engined types.'

'Where would he be based, Mum?' Murray asked.

'Inverness I expect.'

'Good. That means we'll be moving up there, doesn't it? Miles and miles of sandy beach all along the coastline ... I'll be able to sail my model boats every day!' Murray was almost there already.

'Hang on,' I told him. 'We don't know a thing about this job yet. Wait and see what Dad says when he gets in.'

I was typing in an upstairs bedroom when he arrived home. The look on his face didn't tell me much this time.

'How did it all go?'

'W — e —l —l, not sure really.'

Over his late lunch Les explained more. The advantages would be a flying opening at last, no housing problem (accommodation provided in the beautiful Speyside area), good income and reasonable job-security. The disadvantages — having to move and uproot the youngsters from their schools, and uncertainty as to whether the work would prove suitable and satisfying.

'How do you mean?' I asked.

'Well, my biggest query is on the flying side. I'd be required to fly the plane into large international

airports single-handed, and you know how I feel
about manoeuvring small aircraft through such
congested conditions. It's not wise for anyone to handle
that type of flying alone. There's another question mark
in my mind, too. I don't think I'm the right person
for this man. He needs someone to attend to a
hundred and one other tasks connected with his
business. Flying would only be one of several
responsibilities! It's not "me" somehow.'

I can see what Les means. I wouldn't want him
to take this job just for the sake of having
employment. Long-term satisfaction in his work *is*
important.

'I just don't have any feeling of "rightness" about
it,' Les said. 'And I'm not going ahead without that.'

'Is the man waiting on your answer?'

'Yes, I said I'd phone him on Monday. I haven't
come to any final conclusion yet, but I'm pretty sure
it's going to be "no".'

Les's advert ran for three days. We've had no
further responses since yesterday.

'Where does this leave us?' I asked Les, as he
sorted through his employment file.

'Not very much further on. I don't think I'll do
anything about those two salesman jobs I was
offered on Thursday ... I just know I'm not the man
they're needing. But I will follow up this sport's club
possibility.'

'What kind of work is that?'

'Short-term. Involves re-contacting various
individuals who've promised financial backing for
the project. It could lead on to some other opening
with the same set-up. I'll phone on Monday and see if
I can arrange a meeting.'

It's interesting that Les's advert brought four
immediate responses. That looks encouraging. Surely
there'll be something soon.

Monday 5 January
'Horrible, horrible day!' Murray complained at
breakfast. 'I wish term didn't have to start tomorrow.'

'Well, we could cheer up this last day of
the holidays by going into Aberdeen, if you like,' I
suggested. (Last-minute school items were needed
from the shops.)

'Oh *yes*, let's!' the three of them cried.

Les was deep in thought as we cleared away the
dishes and got organized for the trip. I thought I
knew what was coming. I'd been dreading this
moment for him.

'I think I'll call at the Employment Office while
we're in town,' Les said, as casually as if he were
suggesting buying a new shirt. It's a cover-up for all
the turmoil underneath. To him, the fact of having to
draw dole money is the ultimate humiliation. He
never dreamt he would reach such a point. It is
incredibly hard for him — harder than I can ever
know. I've heard people talk in a no-nonsense way
about such things. 'It's only a matter of taking out
what you've already put in!' they insist. It's true, but
Les doesn't find comfort from such facts. As he's told
me so many times over the last ten months: 'I'd far
rather have a job — any job — than apply for
unemployment benefit.'

'Come *on*!' called Stuart. 'When are we going,
Mum?'

Les collected the necessary details from his file,
while I made out a quick shopping-list. Then we were
off.

I tried to think of ways to cheer up Murray's
'horrible day'. There was some cash in my wallet,
sent by Les's aunt 'to buy a special Christmas treat'.
I'd been saving it for the right moment.

'Shall we have lunch out somewhere?'

'Yes, *please*! Where?'

'You choose.'

Rachel was determined to take us to her favourite
eating-place. We trooped in at midday and enjoyed
large hamburgers. We just had room for ice creams
afterwards — bought at the takeaway counter next
door. Everyone selected a different flavour. Sunset

Strip? or Coconut Tropicale? or Chocolate Supreme? or ...?

The youngsters and I bought books with our Christmas tokens while Les went to the Employment Office. We found a 'laughter case' (four volumes). Quite crazy — just what the lads love. It kept them chuckling all the way home. Les and I enjoyed those cartoons together this evening. It was good to hear his genuine amusement. Laughter's a real asset when the going gets rough.

'It will take a while for the office to process my application,' Les told me later. 'I should receive my first payment in about a fortnight.'

'How does it come?'

'Through the post. Just a form which we take to the post office and exchange for cash.'

I'm glad it's done like that. I had unpleasant visions of Les waiting in some long, sordid dole queue at the city office. This way, only our village postmaster will know.

'How much will it be?'

'Not sure yet. I've applied for a rent rebate, too.'

Again, he's so matter-of-fact, giving me the details in as ordinary a way as if we were discussing airline wages. I have to feel my way beneath the surface, trying to understand what's going on inside. Today his distress had been acute, but so carefully and bravely covered over. He did not want to spoil our family fun, or cause the youngsters undue concern. He's determined to be cheerful, to keep interested and involved in all their activities. He will do all he can to prevent his own inner suffering from overshadowing our lives.

I wanted to find the right words to say. Something comforting and strengthening in the middle of all this. I tried out different phrases in my head. They all sounded wrong. Much too glib and superficial. If only I could think of something *right* to say.

'Do you think this income could be God's way of providing for us at present? Just for a short while?'

'Maybe,' Les said slowly. 'But it's going to take me a very long time to see it that way.'

'Why?'

'It seems a come-down after the remarkable ways God provided for us in the past. During our time abroad we were not paid a salary. Our needs then were met in such unexpected ways, filling us with praise. Taking money from the State is altogether different. It makes me ashamed, somehow. I can't see how it can bring honour to God, either. I feel I want to object strongly to him.'

I sat for a long time looking out through the living-room window to the blackness beyond. Silence, except for the faint murmuring of the river. I could see his point, but I couldn't agree. How about other forms of State help — free medical services, subsidized dental care ...? Les avails himself of these without a second thought. But it wasn't the moment to voice my disagreement.

'I wish I could fully understand what it's like for you,' I said.

He smiled. 'I wish you could, too.'

The telephone shrilled, making me jump.

It was Wendy! I'd been eager for the latest news of Simon.

'He's doing surprisingly well,' she told me. 'The bone-marrow test was normal, and he's even back at school. His hair is growing, too.'

'I can't tell you how thrilled we are!'

Simon is still on various drugs, but the doctors are pleased with his good progress. 'It seems as if Simon's illness is definitely in remission,' Wendy said.

'Isn't that great?' I said to Les, after the call. 'Last autumn he was so low I wondered if he'd ever pull through.'

It was good to end this difficult day with happy, encouraging news.

Tuesday 6 January
Each morning I wonder if the postman will bring

that Cambridgeshire letter. There was nothing today. Maybe tomorrow? Les phoned the Speyside man and gave a definite 'no' this morning, before he left for Aberdeen to see the sports-club officials.

I hoped the children weren't feeling too blue, this first day of the new term. Stuart's been put up a class. 'It seems odd to have a son at public school when Dad's drawing dole money,' I thought to myself as I pegged out the washing in an ice-cold wind. We couldn't bear to take him away, though. 'Being stretched academically suits Stuart well!' Les and I have often remarked. The move to a higher class confirms this. I feel sure we won't have to go on paying school fees out of savings much longer. 'Les is sure to find work soon!' I reassured myself. 'It could even be today!'

Les came home at lunch-time, still hopeful about the sports-club possibility.

'But they're going to advertise the post this week,' he told me.

'They'll phone once they've interviewed further applicants.'

Thursday 8 January

The youngsters were grumpy about school when they got in this afternoon. 'I hope there's lots more snow, so the school bus can't run tomorrow!' Rachel said as we gathered at the table for supper. A few flakes were falling already. We sang 'grace': 'Praise God from whom all blessings flow.' An ordinary moment, an ordinary meal — but I was filled with a sudden sense of gratitude. Here we all are, safe, warm, healthy — no more frights with Stuart, provided for. There's sufficient food for this meal, and enough in the larder to supply several more. God's care is very real!

Rachel roped the boys in to help with the washing-up, despite loud protests, while Les and I drove off through the snow for Blackburn. I was showing Ethiopia slides to a small, friendly group of women. Les spent the evening with a friend.

'How did you get on?' I asked as we drove home.

'I appreciated the chance to chat. Bill asked about the employment situation. He advised me to continue looking for a *flying* job. That gives clear guidance in my thinking.'

'What about the sports-club possibility then?'

'I'd take that on a temporary basis, while still looking hard for an opening in aviation.'

'It's interesting how Bill's advice matches what Paul said, all those months ago.'

'Yes. I must confess I've seriously considered chucking up flying lately. The outlook's so bleak. But now I feel inclined to continue.'

I'm pleased about that. I don't want Les to give up hope of getting back on a flight-deck again.

'How did your meeting go?' Les asked.

'I enjoyed it. They were so friendly I was soon put at ease. I didn't feel shy this time!'

Friday 9 January

We woke to bright sunshine, snow dripping from the eaves. Rachel was disgusted.

'It had better snow again next week, preferably late on Sunday,' she muttered.

Les looked longingly out of the kitchen window.

'Perfect day for flying!' he said. 'Air still, sky clear, not a cloud in sight.'

An hour later we saw the sun glinting on a British Airways Trident as it made its final approach to Dyce.

'Know what?' Les said. 'I think I *will* go flying today. I've been wondering about it for a few days now.'

'At the flying-club?'

'Yes. Just to keep my hand in. That's important if I'm offered an interview for the Cambridgeshire post.'

He was suddenly excited. I got a big kick out of watching him fetch his cheque book, licence, log book... He whistled as he went out of the door. Blow the cost! ('Maybe around £20,' Les said.) Today's flying is

important to him in so many ways it will help to
reassure him that he *can* handle an aircraft
competently, despite the previous setbacks. The last
time he stepped off a plane was after that miserable
Base Check. It would be different this time!

The sky was an intense blue as I cycled to the
village. The last few drifts of snow were sparkling.
Marvellous day!

'Where's Dad?' Murray asked, the minute he got
in from school.

'Flying!'

He gave me a quick look of disbelief. 'What do
you mean?' He was not going to be taken in.

'What I said. Dad's taken one of those flying-club
Cessnas up for a spin this afternoon.'

'Wow! Lucky thing!' Rachel cried, coming in
through the back door. The car came into sight
around the corner about 5 p.m. They were waiting to
deluge Dad with questions the moment he stepped
out.

'Was it nice, Dad?' 'Were you sick?' 'How long
did you spend up there?' 'Where did you go?'

'It *was* nice!' Les told them. 'Perfect day for
flying. Peter and I went all round the Grampian
region, mostly up north. The snow on the hills looked
beautiful. It was nice to see the world from that angle
again, too!'

'What did you *do* though?' Murray insisted.

'Lots of different manoeuvres, tight turns, a loop
or two.'

'Were you sick?'

Les hesitated. 'Why do you want to know?'

'That means you were!' the two of them chorused.
'Fancy Dad being sick!'

'You would have been, too. And anyway I wasn't
sick. Just felt a bit green once or twice.'

Later Les told me the cost of one hour's flying:
£40.

'I was horrified, but by then the flight was over. I
had to pay up.'

'You wouldn't have gone on the trip if you'd known the cost beforehand, so I'm glad you didn't,' I said. 'Anyway, the trip certainly wasn't a waste of money. That flight was very important.'

'I guess so.'

The gentleman in Cambridgeshire phoned tonight. He assured Les that his application hasn't been overlooked. Selection of the short list takes place next Monday, and we'll be notified of the result soon afterwards. I'm impressed by their consideration in keeping us well posted, even though they must be swamped with applicants.

'D'you know what Anne said to me yesterday?' I said to Les.

'What?'

'She's sure you're going to be one of the final six!'

'Well, I certainly don't share that feeling,' Les said shortly. 'And anyway, even if I am interviewed, there's only a one-in-six chance of actually getting the job.' He's not counting on anything. My own optimism feels a bit crushed this evening. It will bounce back by tomorrow!

Monday 12 January

Today's the day they decide! During our brief prayer-time this morning I asked God to direct what goes on down there in Cambridgeshire. There was a small brown envelope amongst the letters on the mat. Les opened it and gasped in surprise. 'Look at this!' I could hardly believe my eyes. £40 in cash. No note or name.

'That exactly covers the cost of your flight on Friday!' God *does* still have exciting ways of providing for us.

'I don't like to accept it,' Les said. 'But I guess we've no choice.' He looked solemn, but I knew he was happy and grateful underneath.

'I'd love to know who sent it!' I said.

'Could be one of any number of friends,' Les answered. 'The postmark is Aberdeen.'

That gift has made my day. It's the second of two anonymous cash receipts this month. I only wish we could thank the donor. It's a humbling experience to receive in such a way.

Wednesday 14 January

'Mum, when am I going to be able to ride my bike again?' Stuart asked over his quick, early breakfast.

'Soon, I hope. I can't think you'll need to be restricted for much longer.'

'What was wrong with me in November, then?'

He's asked that question so many times. It's obviously on his mind.

'Just a choke, I think. Only a few days now till you see the specialist.'

There was still no word from the sports club. They should phone soon if they're still interested in Les. He tried making contact with their office after breakfast. No result. The boss was out, not likely to be back for several hours.

The letter-box clicked. A letter with a Cambridgeshire postmark! Les was reading upstairs, so I rushed up to give it to him. He was as calm and steady as ever. He unfolded the letter, read down the page, then said 'Well, fancy that!'

'What?'

'I've been short-listed!'

'Marvellous!' I burst out. I wanted to shout it from the roof-top! Fantastic! Les studied the delight written all over my face. He smiled back quickly, then said 'We'll need to talk this one through.'

'How do you mean?' Nothing's going to crush my optimism this time!

'Well, now there *is* a remote, one-in-six chance I might be offered the job ...'

'Yes?'

'... what would I do? Accept or not?'

'Accept, of course!'

'But have you stopped to consider all that would mean?'

'Not in detail. I just want you to get a good, satisfying flying job. The rest will probably fall into place.'

'Will it?'

We stood by the bedroom window, overlooking the angry grey river — swollen by melting snow from the hills. Les confronted me with the stark, unwelcome facts. What about accommodation? We'd never find another house like this, at such a reasonable rent. Purchase was out of the question now. And schools? Could we bear to move Stuart, or interrupt Rachel's important 'Higher Grade' exam year? What about leaving friends, responsibilities at the church, etc., etc.? Les spelt it all out, taking his usual matter-of-fact approach. Underneath he's torn in two. He'd welcome that interesting flying job. Plenty of scope for the future, too, it seems. But what about the inevitable trauma of uprooting everyone? Is it fair? The alternatives churn round and round in his mind.

'Yes, moving would be hard. No question about it. But your work tops the priority list as far as I'm concerned. I'd be willing to sacrifice almost anything to see you happy and fulfilled once more. I can't bear the problem to drag on like this.'

'We can stall on it for the moment, anyway,' Les said. 'I haven't even been offered the job yet.' He rummaged in the cupboard for his old trousers. 'I must check the car's starter motor. That could be why it's refusing to budge these mornings.'

I walked along to the village. The river-side route is still a delight, even though the tall reeds are now brown and broken, and old rose hips hang shrivelled from the tangled bushes. Empty broom pods rattle in the faint breeze. A swan family dabbled below the village bridge. I was quick to respond to the loveliness of it all, even in mid-winter. The prospect of leaving saddens me. It's easy to say 'I'd willingly sacrifice almost anything ...' but do I really feel that way?

I thought about it while I lingered on the river-bank, remembering the increasing strain and anguish over all these long months — nearly a year now. I saw again the despair which sometimes crosses Les's face. 'Anything, even a move south, if it's going to relieve all that,' I told myself — and I meant it. Perhaps I could remain here with the youngsters till Rachel's exams were over? Murray hasn't even begun his O-level subjects, so a move won't make much difference to him. And Stuart can always stay on later as a boarder. It's not so complicated as it seemed earlier. We'd soon find new friends and church responsibilities, too, though the parting here would be hard.

Thursday 15 January

The first unemployment benefit cheque came with the morning post (£99.80 per fortnight). The postman deserves a medal for getting through to us! There's been a blizzard all night, and the snow is now very deep.

'Eighteen inches!' yelled Murray, from the centre of the lawn. He couldn't wait to get out there with Dad's steel measuring-tape. Murray and Rachel are delighted at missing school.

'The bus won't make it tomorrow, either,' Rachel predicted. 'That means four days off in a row, counting the weekend.' Stuart's Aberdeen bus operates, whatever the weather.

Murray found a shovel to clear the outside path. Progress was slow. The council workers passed, pushing the pavement snow aside with a small mechanized plough. Large ploughs and gritting lorries were busy, too. I'd be able to walk to the village by mid-morning and cash the benefit cheque. That should help towards meeting the heavy electricity bill (over £100 this quarter) and phone expenses.

This afternoon I realized that depression can decend like a bolt out of the blue. I was cheerful and busy all morning, then suddenly overwhelmed by circumstances during the after-lunch lull. Not completely without warning, though. The hopefulness of New Year's Day is being steadily overshadowed by the strain of living with continued uncertainty. I feel I *must* know what's going to happen. The pain I feel for Les hurts so much sometimes. There's a limit to endurance. Surely the longed-for breakthrough will come soon?

But will it? Sitting in an upstairs bedroom, looking out over the bleak, wintry scene (it seems to reflect our own hard struggle) I tried to remind myself of the truth God showed so clearly way back in October — that twig caught in the river-side reeds

I leant back against the armchair, deliberately relaxing each tense muscle. I had to force myself into physical rest in order to be open to mental and spiritual calm. It worked! — slowly. I became less taut. Familiar Bible words crept into my mind: 'My grace is all you need, for my power is strongest when you are weak.' I lingered on that sentence. Today's sense of utter helplessness and frustration can lead me again to God's gift of trust. And trust, in turn, can help release me from the grip of depression, despite family circumstances.

Rachel burst in. 'Here you are! Dad's made a pot of tea. Murray and I are going sledging. See you at supper-time!'

I was glad of the brief chance to unwind and think more clearly. I feel much better now.

Saturday 17 January
Today I was willing to appreciate winter once more. Crisp snow glistened in the sunlight as Les and I walked beside the river. The water level was lower, but it will rise rapidly when the thaw begins. Midstream rocks were skull-capped in white; gulls circled above steel-blue water. January has its own brief, sombre beauty.

'This time next week you'll be on your way to Cambridgeshire!' I said to Les. He's arranged to spend the weekend with Mother. 'When will you be back?'

'Let's think. I'm seeing round the place all day Monday, then interviews on Tuesday, so it could be some time Wednesday.' That sounds exciting. Only another week to go!

We walked along the top of the flood-bank for a while.

'I might try phoning that company at Dyce this afternoon. I wouldn't want to miss anything that's going.'

'Is this the flying possibility James mentioned?'

'Yes, he's been asking around for me.'

Les phoned as soon as we got back.

'Sorry, the crew vacancies have already been filled,' they said.

'So it's nothing doing there, after all,' Les sighed. 'I sometimes wonder if they ever stop to look through their files.'

'Has that company already got your details, then?'

'Yes, I've filled in application forms for all the local groups.'

There was the usual Saturday muddle of activity in the kitchen. Rachel was cutting out new 'cords' on the working-space. Murray was fitting a mast to his yacht, with the hull lodged firmly in the plate-rack. Stuart was testing his tug-boat batteries in the socket beside the bread-bin. Not an inch of space for supper preparations! But I was glad to see them occupied — it stops them bickering!

Monday 19 January

The day for Stuart's appointment with the specialist — at last! Les drove him to hospital. The consultant was reassuring. 'Probably just a choke.' He ordered several tests as a safeguard. 'We might as well do an electrocardiogram, too' he said. Everything was complete by midday, so Les was home soon afterwards. The results will be sent to our doctor within a fortnight. No problems anticipated. It's a relief that it's all so straightforward. Not that we've been worried. Stuart's as fit and flourishing as ever! He'll be thrilled to ride his bike again.

Tuesday 20 January

At the beginning of each fortnight Les has to fill in an unemployment benefit claim form. It needs to be signed by a householder. I took today's round to Anne this morning. It saves Les the embarrassment of having to ask. Not that he'd show it. But it must be irksome to him. The form caught the 11.30 a.m. post. The cheque should be back on Friday.

While I was gone Les listed several UK flying companies on a sheet of paper. 'I feel I must phone as many of these as possible and sound out the possibilities of getting work during the coming months,' he explained later. 'I want to know the score all round before I go to Cambridgeshire.'

I bought haddock from the fish van this morning. So fresh they almost winked up at me from the chopping-board. Caught, sold, and cooked for lunch within the space of hours. Delicious!

'How did it all go?' I asked Les over the meal.

'It didn't. Not a thing to offer. The outlook couldn't be more depressing.'

'Even with spring and summer ahead?'

'Yes. That's what makes it worse. One chief pilot down south told me that he has 400 applicants on file — I'm one of them — and that approximately 1,000 pilots are now looking for work. It makes you wonder if there's any point at all in trying further.'

'That makes this Cambridgeshire opening all the more crucial.'

'It's all I've got now.'

Wednesday 21 January

A quick shopping trip into Aberdeen this afternoon. We drove back at dusk (3.30 p.m.) — the sky an intense gold; air shining, still; wisps of grey mist weaving between cold trees. A fluffed-out pheasant strutted across the smooth snow — ridiculously conspicuous!

Everywhere calm, a penetrating peace, easing the constant strain of circumstance. I felt as a child must, when stilled against its mother's breast. It was good to grasp at this moment of refreshment. It helps to compensate for the long absence of a break or holiday.

Thursday 22 January

These empty, seemingly pointless, days must be so tedious for Les. I've been trying to think of different ways to fill the long hours. Today's been an 'entertaining' day — rather female orientated. Sandra came for coffee. Her usual jolly self. Lots of laughs. At midday we drove to Inverurie, picked up Annette from her sheltered workshop, and brought her back for lunch. She looked tired and worn, worse than when we last saw her in the autumn. (She has multiple sclerosis — there's no cure — and she's so young.) I watched her faltering steps through our doorway and into the hall. I didn't offer an arm: she fiercely guards her remaining independence. I can understand. It could have been me. I reached out a hand as she stumbled, then steadied herself again, and I suddenly felt a deep bond with Annette in her suffering. I hope she senses my caring, though I can't find words to express it.

'Nice smell of lunch!' she smiled. 'Oh, and you've got a cat!' I watched her sink on to the fireside rug beside 'Miss Puss', then got busy with last-minute meal preparations.

I was glad Annette could spend her brief lunch-hour with us. I didn't like to suggest driving back to the workshop. She looked so comfortable down there by the fire. 'I prefer it to a chair!'

'If only you didn't live so far away,' I said later as Les drove us over the hill towards Inverurie. (Annette's home is about thirty-five miles away in a small fishing village.)

'Never mind, I might come across in my car one day,' she said.

'Yes, do!'

'Not that I like lonely country roads,' Annette added. 'It's no joke getting stuck miles from anywhere.' There was a sad, anxious note in her voice. How I wish there was more we could do.

We left her at the workshop. She waved briefly, then walked slowly though the main door. We drove across country to the egg farm for our monthly order. Benachie was jagged black now, against the reddening sky.

'Do you think there's time to visit Miss Duncan?' I asked Les.

'Just about.'

We called in at the hospital on the way home. I always welcome a chance to see Miss D. She must be eighty-nine now, though she hopes I don't know.

'I hear you're going home tomorrow!' I breezed in.

Her pale blue eyes suddenly brimmed with tears. 'I want to go Home so much,' she said. 'But only God can take me there.'

She's never sad for long, though. We were soon laughing about various happenings on the ward. She has a delightful sense of humour, eyes twinkling. Her smile does me a world of good. She hated to see us go. 'They won't even let me come out to the car here,' she complained.

'Never mind. You'll be back in your own little flat tomorrow!' I reminded her.

'Oh, *yes*! I hope my azalea's still bonnie, and my amaryllis, and my rose, and my new cactus ...'

Friday 23 January
Les and I cycled up to the village together this morning. We collected *Flight* from the newsagent.

'Anything yet?' I asked.

'Nothing.'

We made a detour through Fetternear on the way home. Trees still gaunt, tall thin ghosts of last summer's splendour. This time next week we'll know the score on the Cambridgeshire post. I can't wait!

Saturday 24 January
It was dark outside as Les and I ate a quick breakfast. Just an hour to spare before the train left,

as we scraped ice from the car windscreen.

'I hope it starts,' Les muttered.

It didn't. There were groans and shudders with each turn of the ignition key.

'Can't think what's wrong now. The motor's working fine,' Les said. Then, 'You get in behind the wheel, I'll push!'

His feet slipped and slid on the icy road. The car was stubborn as ever. What now? He couldn't miss that train.

'Let's try once more!' called Les. I steered round the first bend.

'Let your foot off *now*!'

The car faltered, then decided to co-operate at last. Les leapt in beside me. We were off!

'Got everything?' I asked.

'Hope so. I checked my brief case again this morning.'

I'm so excited for Les. I feel almost sure he's heading for success this time. Even the offer of an interview is tremendous. It must have been a big boost to Les's morale. I'm proud of him!

'Don't use the car again this weekend,' Les told me. 'Starting problems must be due to that old battery after all. I'll look for a new one when I get back.'

'Are they expensive?'

'£30 or so.'

The roads were almost empty at this early hour. We soon reached the station.

'Don't wait!' Les said, collecting his case from the boot. Next time I see him we'll know the outcome — yes or no. It's got to be a 'yes'!

The rising sun was a brilliant gold, promising to be a beautiful day. Spring is almost here. Good, I'm fed up with winter! The car was willing to take me into Inverurie this afternoon without a murmur of protest. I spent an hour at a women's all-day Prayer Conference. I glanced round during the first hymn — mostly strangers. Everyone began to clasp hands.

Women on either side took mine. It was quite
unexpected and unfamiliar to me, but comforting,
too. They knew nothing of our circumstances, yet
their touch strengthened me. I'm so hesitant to
express concern for others in a physical way. Maybe I
need to rediscover the special value of a caring touch?

Sunday 25 January
The weekend has gone well. It's seemed strange without
Les, though. I've got so used to having him at home.
He phoned at tea-time, enjoying the break at
Mother's. It was frosty out tonight. As I made my
way up the steep hill to the church hall for the
minister's discussion group, I paused to look up at
the starry sky. Magnificent! 'Fancy, the Maker of all
that has our affairs in hand, too!'

Monday 26 January
I had lots of time to think of Les as I busied myself
with the Monday chores. He'd enjoy seeing round the
airport. Might even take the plane up, too. I like the
sound of this group. They'd be good people to work
for. A new thought struck me. Today I must pray for
them — to find the right man for their needs — Les,
or whoever. Aren't the affairs of all men ultimately
in God's hands? So requesting or expecting a
personal favour at the possible cost of another's well-
being must be to disregard the wider circle of God's
concern.

The phone rang again at lunch-time — the third
call in two hours. It was Maureen.

'Just wanted to let you know we're thinking of
Les, and praying, too!'

Another friend who's right with us at present. I
felt touched and grateful for this detailed concern. By
Wednesday we could be phoning them all back to
share good news! The thought of this increased my
excitement.

Tuesday 27 January
'Dad's got his interview today, hasn't he?' Stuart

asked, gulping down a mug of tea before racing for
the bus.

'Yes.'

'So he'll know whether he's got the job or not by
this evening?'

'I expect so.'

'Great! I'm sure he'll be picked. Can I tell my
friends at school?'

'Hang on, lad! Mustn't count on anything yet. We
could be disappointed.'

He dashed out of the front door, heavy school-
bag thumping against his back. I heard him
whistling happily down the street.

The interview was scheduled for 11.30. My
thoughts became quick prayers as the morning
progressed. I value this link-up when I can't be there
myself. 11.30. 11.45. Midday. He should be getting
near the end of the interview now. I sat down with
soup and sandwiches and a large American apple.
Imagine them sending a consignment all this way, to
our small Aberdeenshire village store!

1.15. The phone rang. Les! A quick call-box
message.

'I'm on my way home, arriving 9.45 tonight.'

'How did you get on?'

'Fair.'

'Any result?'

'No.'

The pips interrupted and we were cut off.

So he didn't know yet? How disappointing. I felt
sure they'd give him the score straight away. How
much longer will we have to wait? It had taken the
keen edge off my excitement. I sat slowly slicing up
that bright red American apple. Well, at least it's not
a 'no' ... Then I suddenly remembered that the
country buses don't run after 8 p.m. How was Les
going to get home? I'd have to meet him with the car.
But how? I hadn't used it for four days. The battery
would be completely dead. And it was no good trying

to charge it. 'The old thing won't even respond to that now,' Les had told me last week.

I decided to go out and turn the ignition, all the same. It might co-operate. But no, not even a flicker of engine life. It must have finally died over the past few days. The street was empty, everyone at work. No point in looking around for help. I walked slowly back into the house. Now what?

'Lord, can you help me to get that thing going?' I asked. It seemed rather an ordinary request, but it mattered a lot to me. I decided to wait an hour, then try again. I might have flooded the engine.

At 4 p.m. I walked back to the car and climbed in. 'Hey, what's that?' I frowned at the very old, very dirty battery on the car floor beside the passenger seat. 'Where's it come from? How did it get there?' I sat puzzling for few seconds. A sudden thought occurred to me. 'Don't be stupid. How could it be *our* battery?' I couldn't resist peeping under the bonnet all the same. What? No! I must be seeing things. I *am* seeing things — a brand-new battery, installed and ready for use. Flabbergasted!

Who? How? When? 'Oh God, you're fantastic! Now I *will* be able to meet Les, after all.' (He'd be so tired after his long journey.) I jumped back behind the wheel and turned the ignition. The engine surged to life after a brief hesitation. It hasn't sounded so healthy for months! As I walked through the front door and into the living room, still stunned, Murray arrived home from school.

'I found this note on the mat!'

I slit open the envelope and read, 'A new battery has been fitted to your car. The old one is beside the passenger seat. Please accept this replacement as a gift.' No name; writing unfamiliar.

'What's the excitement, Mum?' The words tumbled out as I told him the whole story. I had to repeat it again for Rachel, and for Stuart.

'If only I knew who'd bought and fitted it!' I said. 'I would just love to let them know how grateful I feel. It's nothing short of a miracle. And to think they've given it on the very day when I needed the car most!'

At supper-time our 'grace' included special appreciation for the battery. I shall just have to accept this expensive gift with gratitude. Full stop. No probing to discover the donor, who has chosen to be anonymous. It's hard to receive on such terms, though. I feel such a debt.

At 9 p.m. I set off for the station. The car started first go. What a treat! It was foggy and the train was delayed, arriving at 10.20. I saw Les coming from far down the platform. He looked weary.

'You drive!' I told him. I couldn't wait to see Les's face when he turned the ignition!

'Hope it starts!' he muttered.

The car burst into life, engine purring happily. Les turned to me in amazement.

'What's happened?'

'You'll never guess ...'

I repeated the long exciting story for the fourth time. It was fun to tell him, as we drove back through dark, foggy lanes. Les was stunned, too. I could tell he was finding it hard to accept such a gift. I knew the feeling!

'Now, what about the interview?' I asked.

'Not much to report. They'll be writing soon. So we'll just have to wait on that letter.'

'How long?'

'Don't know. Maybe a week.'

That long. I'd hoped we'd hear by Saturday at the very latest. (Optimism makes me inclined to impatience.) Les was being rather cagey about the whole affair. Why? Everything about this job had seemed so good.

'Did you click with things down there?'

'Sort of. But I'm not nearly as keen as I was.'

His words came as a shock.

'Why?'

Then he explained the situation in detail. The big

drawback is lack of job security. I never anticipated this. The programme could be wound down within the next two years. The new pilot is expected clearly to understand this before accepting the post.

'So I could find myself out of work again,' Les went on. 'And it certainly wouldn't be easy to find something else in aviation in that area. Far better to hang on up here where things should eventually pick up.'

So he's not inclined to go, even if the interview is successful. It came as a painful blow. I can't quite take it in yet. My optimism is crushed again.

'Housing would be another difficulty,' I heard Les say. 'I looked at a few agents' adverts. Purchase is out of the question. And rented property is almost impossible to obtain in that area. We don't know how fortunate we are up here.'

There was a long, empty silence. A scattering of blurred lights came into view round the bend by the village golf course. I was trying to understand Les's reasoning, but it wasn't easy. Les sensed my bewilderment.

'Don't worry. I haven't made any decision yet, of course. We'll just have to wait and see what their letter says. It could be a "no" anyway.'

Wednesday 25 January

Les tried getting in touch with the sports club again this morning.

'Sorry, the manager is out,' the secretary told him. The same response each time.

'Not much point in trying any more,' Les sighed. 'They're obviously not interested.' I suppose he's right. It's over three weeks since his visit to them.

'Nothing at all in the pipeline now,' Les said, half to himself.

'You've still got the Cambridgeshire possibility.'

'Yes, but I'm not too hopeful. I think they're going to take the other chap I met. He seemed more suited to the job.'

Les sat dejectedly at the dining-table, head in

hands. I could guess what he was thinking; '*Must* get work. Anything. Should I try advertising again? Or shall I contact all those city agencies? I could even write to several more flying companies in the *Operator's Directory*.'

He got up to fetch his file, the latest copy of *Flight*, the typewriter — forcing himself to *do* something, trying to work up enough determination to counteract the growing frustration. He's only interested in flying really, yet he knows he must now take anything. I hoped he sensed how much I feel for him in all of this. There was not much I could say as I stood peeling apples for a supper crumble. But I care deeply.

Thursday 29 January

This morning I called in at the surgery to renew a prescription. The doctor called me to his room. 'I want to talk to you about Stuart.'

'Yes? Have the test results come through?'

'They have. All quite normal, except for one.' I was startled by the seriousness of his voice. I could feel my face getting hot. 'It seems that Stuart's heart stopped beating during that crisis in November.'

I stiffened. 'What does that mean?'

'Well, there's some kind of heart irregularity. Needs further investigation. I can't give you any more information than that at present.'

'Is it serious?'

'I don't know. We'll get a heart specialist to see him. The hospital will send an appointment soon.'

He was helpful and considerate. I valued his calm approach. 'Don't tell Stuart,' he said.

Out in the cold, wet street my head started to spin. It *can't* be. They must have got it wrong. A young healthy lad like Stuart can't have heart trouble. No. It's impossible.

I met our minister in the post office and felt I must tell someone. He listened with concern, tried to reassure me. How glad I was of his understanding.

Cycling home, I met Les halfway.

'Just going to paint the cupboards at the church hall,' he said. Then 'What's up?' Slowly I told him. I hated having to do it — to see the deep, troubled look in his eyes. It's one thing to bear our own load of difficulty — quite another to know that our son is faced with a problem we may not be able to solve or remove. This is much harder.

'I'll go on up to the hall now,' Les said at last, wanting to be alone with his thoughts.

'See you at lunch-time, then!' My cheerfulness sounded hollow.

I pedalled home against the biting wind and put my bike away in the large hall cupboard. Standing there, I was suddenly overwhelmed by fear. The implications of this situation hit me full force. What caused that cardiac arrest? What if it happens again? Suppose Stuart is alone in the street, or on a bus? Will people know what to do? He was so hard to resuscitate last time. I saw that nightmare scene once more — his wide vacant eyes, blue cheeks, flaccid limbs. No, it just can't happen again. I couldn't bear it.

My mind in a turmoil, thoughts running wild, I went into the kitchen, made coffee, then sat drinking it at the dining-table. We can only trust God's mercy in this situation. There's little we can do to protect Stuart. We can't wrap him round with restrictions, smother him with 'suppose-it-happens' precautions. That's just not possible, or advisable.

'Haven't we always assumed that God will take care of our children?' I asked myself. 'All right, now we've got to put that into practice.' It will mean letting him go off in the dark at 7.30 each morning without tensing up and worrying all day about the frightening possibilities. That's hard; very hard. Can we do it?

Friday 30 January

'Bye everyone!' yelled Stuart at 7.25 a.m. He was just off for the bus, oblivious of our anxiety. He hasn't a clue what's up.

'My, it's hard to let him go now, isn't it?' I said to Les, as we began our usual time of Bible reading and prayer together upstairs.

'Yes,' he answered, deep in thought.

This is the moment when all that theory about 'God keeping them' has to become real, or I'll end up a nervous wreck.

'We can think of him specially in our prayers this morning,' Les said. 'Doing that every day will help us to get through this rough patch.'

There was a long empty day ahead for Les. He thought he might spend an hour finishing off the cupboards at the hall.

'Let's talk about the work situation before you start the chores,' Les suggested, when breakfast was over and Rachel and Murray had been hustled off to school.

'Maybe the postman will bring word from Cambridgeshire?' I began.

'I doubt it. I don't expect to hear for another week.'

There was silence for a while. Les knows I'm still keen on that possibility. He hesitated, trying to find right words.

'I've made up my mind about the flying post down there,' he began. 'I just don't feel right about it at all ...'

'Yes?'

'... so even if they offer me the job, I won't take it.'

So that was that. It was all over. Another door gone bang. No good saying anything. Les had made up his mind. And if I'm going to trust him I need to accept that decision. I'm finding that trust isn't always an easy, natural reaction. It sometimes needs will-power.

'I see,' I answered slowly. 'At least I know where we are now. No need to think further about changing the youngsters' schooling, or moving away from this lovely part of the country.'

'No. I think I'll go all out to find something local instead. I'll try every possible line, as well as keeping up with flying possibilities which wouldn't involve a move. I should find something soon. I'll go and get some advice from the agencies next week.'

Les was forcing himself into uncharacteristic optimism for my sake. He hates to see the disappointment on my face. I'm touched by his consideration. They say that trouble makes or breaks a marriage. This long problem is certainly strengthening the bonds between us.

Month 13

Sunday 1 February

Goodbye to January! I was glad to rip the first month off the new calendars. It was over.

'It won't be too much longer now before Les's problems end!' That's what friends often tell us. I always smile and agree when they say it. I want them to know their optimism is appreciated.

We had long hours of brilliant sunshine today. There is a faint haze of new green across on the far river-bank. So spring really is pushing old winter aside!

Less happens on Sundays. There's more time to think. And today my thoughts centred on Stuart again. I have to remind myself all the time that God sees and cares for Stuart. Will I let myself take rest in that?

Monday 2 February

I hoped the postman would bring the first replies to the job enquiry letters Les posted last Wednesday. But there was only one letter on the mat this morning. An airform from Sri Lanka. I couldn't think who could have sent it. The name was unfamiliar, the request carefully typed. It was from a Sri Lankan evangelist, an older, retired man, desperately needing funds to pay travel expenses from place to place. He obtained my name and address from the bottom of a magazine article. It's a sad letter. I can't help feeling for him. What should I do?

'No good sending money. It won't benefit him in the long run,' Les cautioned.

'It seems wrong not to do something, though.' I shall put the letter aside for a while. I need time to think this one through.

Stuart is fit and flourishing. He's even keen on school these days. He's keeping up in the new class and getting good marks. I hope the specialist appointment comes through soon.

Tuesday 3 February
Margaret arrived from Monymusk this afternoon and stopped for a fly-cup. Farm life is chilly and bleak these days, though the weekend sunshine was welcome.

'Frank's got a buyer for last year's potato crop at last,' Margaret told me. 'So this week we'll be sorting and bagging "tatties". Do you think Les would like to help? I warn you, it's hard work.'

'Oh, he won't mind that. I'm sure he'd be glad of something to do!'

Les was quite keen when I told him afterwards. He's glad of a chance to reduce the unemployment benefit by taking in some earnings. (Frank insists on paying him.) He put his old workshop overalls and gloves ready this evening. He'll start at the farm tomorrow.

'I meant to tell you I've put another "Situations Wanted" advert in the local paper,' Les told me. 'It might come out tomorrow. Just note the details from anyone who phones.'

Wednesday 4 February
I still keep looking for that Cambridgeshire letter — or any other job replies — each time the postman calls. If only he knew how we watch and wait for his arrival every morning! Nothing again today.

Les was off at 8.30 a.m. Margaret's kindly giving
him lunch — he'll enjoy her delicious cooking. He
expected to be home around 4.15.

I decided to answer the Sri Lanka letter. I was
tempted to send financial help, but then realized that
the evangelist's own small church (mentioned by
him) needs to accept this responsibility. They will
never have the opportunity to do so if funds are
always sought from abroad.

'Suppose one of our youngsters badly needed
something, but went next door to ask, rather than
coming first to us?' I thought to myself. 'Something
would be badly wrong.' I tried to explain my point of
view in the letter. I hope it doesn't sound cold and
uncaring.

As the family started arriving back from school,
Les came in, exhausted.

'Just shows how flabby my muscles are getting!'
he said. 'Any phone calls?'

'No.'

'Well, the advert's definitely in today's paper. I
saw it at the Black's.' We were just about to sit down
to a home-cooked fish-and-chip supper when the
phone rang. I lifted the receiver.

'May I speak to the airline pilot who's
advertising in today's paper?' asked a gentleman
with a thick Scots accent. My hopes shot sky-high!

'Yes, certainly. I'll call him.'

Les took the call, while the rest of us crowded
round, all ears.

'Yes, I'm qualified to fly a Cessna 210,' we heard
him say. Then, 'Where's the job? Sutherland?' The
youngsters and I exchanged excited smiles. It
sounded really good! Was this our breakthrough, at
last?

'Certainly, I'd be glad to meet and discuss further
details. But who did you say your colleague is?
Donald McRae?'

There was a brief silence. Then Les burst into
laughter.

'Donald, you old rogue! You gave it away by using your name like that. And what's this spiel about a Cessna crop-spraying in Sutherland? You really baffled me there. Never heard of a 210 doing that before!'

It was all a hoax, executed to perfection by mischievous Don, a final-year student in Aberdeen, who hasn't been in touch for months. I didn't know whether to smile or not. There was such sad irony in Don's joke. But Les laughed it off with genuine amusement. It didn't rankle with him at all. How I admire him for that.

'Didn't Don put on a stunning accent?' he chuckled. 'Oh, and I've asked him out this Saturday. That's all right isn't it? Just wait till I see him!'

Friday 6 February
I kept Stuart home from school today. He said he was feeling dizzy, and he has a cold. Usually I toss such minor complaints off with a casual 'You'll soon be fine!'. No question of missing lessons and staying in bed. It was different this time and Stuart was surprised.

'It's not that bad, Mum!'

'Yes, I know. But I think we'd better play safe after last November.'

'Why? That's not going to happen again, is it?'

'I don't think so. Anyway, just sit back and enjoy a day off school. You're missing a chilly afternoon on the games field, aren't you?' For all his protests, I think he's enjoyed a bit of fuss from Mum.

The last day of the advert. No response at all this time. It seems odd after getting four calls before.

'That sets me back about £9,' Les said late this evening. 'I guess I'll need to think up another line of attack.'

'You haven't been to the agencies yet, have you?'

'No, I'll spend a day in town once the "tattie bagging" is over.'

He paused for a few moments, spooning out the

cocoa dregs from the bottom of his mug.

'What *is* God trying to show me through all of this? If only he'd make it clear. Why does he keep me waiting week after week?'

I have no answer. I'm asking the same questions.

'I just don't know. It seems like some long, tedious test – and painful. If I didn't know that the Person who's allowing this wretched experience is trustworthy, I'd have given up long ago. Trust seems all we've got to go on, doesn't it?'

I suppose so. Mine's wearing a bit thin at present. I need something positive to happen by way of encouragement.'

At moments like this the pain surges back. Most of the time I can keep it at bay deliberately filling each day's programme with activity. But the anguish can't be held in check for long. I feel it for Les, not myself. If only this were *my* pain. That would make it so much easier to bear.

My mind went back to the battery gift of ten days ago. (The car is in excellent form now!) That gave my trust a tremendous boost. Should I remind Les of it, to try to lift his spirits? It needed to be put carefully.

'But God *is* acting positively, isn't he? Like when he prompted someone to buy and fit that battery?'

'Yes, true enough. But I'm looking for something positive in the work line. That's of prime importance. Once I'm earning, we'll be able to provide what we need for the car and everything else ourselves.'

Les got up and let the cat in, then locked the doors. 'I must get to bed.' He's very weary after working at the farm all week. Seems to be getting another boil, too.

Saturday 7 February

Donald joined us for lunch today. He looked sheepish as he walked in. He needn't have worried. Les couldn't think of a suitable way to 'punish' him for that hoax! It was bitterly cold this afternoon. Donald and Les drove the boys to Monymusk lake for more model-boat trials. It was no go; the water was frozen.

'Even the swans were skating!' Donald reported,
when they returned.

The boys amused themselves with a large empty
plastic bottle instead. They filled it with water, then
pumped in air till the whole thing looked dangerously
bloated.

'Take it outside — immediately!' I insisted.

They disappeared for a few minutes. Then there
were ominous thuds and shrieks of glee. Murray burst
in.

'You should have seen my water bomb, Mum!
Shot right up over the house, then came down again
in a fantastic spray. There's soapy water everywhere!'

Boys!

Monday 9 February

Tattie-bagging should be completed today. The
postman arrived after Les had left. That
Cambridgeshire letter, at last! I was dying to read it,
but Les must see it first. I propped it up on the
sideboard, for him to see as soon as he got in. I was
still keen on this possibility. Suppose they *were*
writing to offer Les the post? Would he change his
mind?

'That letter's come!' I called out as soon as Les
walked in at the front door.

'What letter?'

'From Cambridgeshire, of course!'

Les didn't seem at all excited. He opened it
slowly, and scanned the contents. It looked like quite
a long letter. Must be a 'yes'! They wouldn't write all
that for a 'no'.

'You can read it,' Les said, handing the page to
me.

The tone of the letter was business-like, but
friendly. They regret that Les's application has not
been successful, though they wish to thank him for
his interest, and trust that he will soon obtain
alternative employment in the aviation industry.

'That confirms my decision, doesn't it?'

'Yes.'

Now I've got to accept that the door really has

slammed shut. It's no good yearning for what lies on the other side. It's not for Les. Didn't I ask God to give them the right person to meet their needs?

I heard Stuart coming in. Everyone was home. I must serve supper. The living-room door opened. Stuart paused before dumping his heavy school-bags on the floor. His face was very pale. He looked exhausted — and it's only the beginning of the week.

'Everything all right?' I asked.

'Yes.' He flopped into an armchair, while I served spaghetti bolognese.

Late tonight I checked the boys' room. I've made a habit of it since November. Both lads were sound asleep. I paused in the doorway, anxiety for Stuart suddenly pulling me up with a start. I didn't think we should send him off to school each day until after the specialist's appointment. It seemed too risky. I put my thoughts to Les.

'I know how you feel,' he began, 'but we can't do that. Much better to let the lad carry on as normal. We don't want to worry him unnecessarily.'

He's right, of course. I'm being thrown back on trust again. It's hard.

Tuesday 10 February

Les's help is in demand. He's begun tattie-bagging at another Monymusk farm today. My treatment seems to be slowly winning with that boil, too. I hope he doesn't get any more. 'They always come when I'm strung up about something,' Les said. He staggered in with a huge sack tonight – one hundredweight of potatoes, as a gift from the farm. Big ones, too! Most thoughtful of them.

'Can we have chips tonight?' Murray asked, picking out several of the largest tatties. He helped me peel and chop.

'About a week's more work at this other farm,' Les told me.

Saturday 14 February

Sunshine woke me at 7.45 a.m. What a joy after the long dark winter mornings! I heard the call of wild geese overhead. So they're on the move, too. Spring really is bursting in. The beech trees are gold in the gleaming sunlight, a faint patch of green on the ground beneath their tangled roots. What a welcome sight! I hope we're heading for a 'spring' in our own circumstances, too.

8.30 a.m. A pair of Whooper swans flew upriver, the steady beat of wings clearly to be heard despite the morning noises all around.

Les and I cycled the Craigearn route this afternoon, beckoned out by the loveliness of it all. Fields and hedgerows are still recovering from the drab winter. No flowers yet. Fat maternal ewes nibbled the tired grass. The field by the river was full of white birds. Rather far off. Were they wild geese, too?

Monday 16 February

Stuart's appointment has arrived! This coming Thursday, at 2 p.m. Good, we won't have to wait much longer.

Dreary rain all morning. I spent time on the household accounts over my midday snack. Less than £40 in the bank account at present. I suddenly felt very afraid. I hadn't realized the balance was so low. What are we going to do? Dip into savings again? Fear grows, penetrating deep into my thinking. No good kidding myself that we're managing. We're not. But where can I economize now? Reducing the food bills by buying even less meat (just mince and sausages), vegetables, fruit, snacks (like crisps) makes only a minimal difference. The cuts need to be much bigger.

The car is the worst culprit. It gulps down gallons of petrol these days. We can try using it less. It's good weather for cycling now. I can keep the clothes' bills down, too. The boys are quite happy with one pair of shoes each, and shouldn't need any other expensive items till autumn. Rachel is getting a kick out of making her own clothes now. Her new skirt's very smart.

I decided that the total expenditure for the week must not exceed £22. (The cost of living is higher in Scotland than in many other parts of Britain.) I'll try to keep within this limit without getting strung up if extra funds are needed sometimes. I flicked over the pages of the fat black accounts book. I've been using it for fifteen years now. It bears record to the fact that we've never lacked basic necessities, and have often enjoyed unexpected extras. Looking back over entries made in Ethiopia and Nairobi (29 Oct. 1965: gift of two chickens; 1 May 1973: two special contributions towards support - £200) I found fear receding. It hasn't gone, but isn't swamping me now. Aren't we still in God's hands, as much today as when I first began these records?

A young couple - Alex and Fiona - called unexpectedly this evening. We enjoyed getting to know them. They were married last summer and are now trying to complete university studies. We discovered that they've been given notice to leave their present bed-sitter in six weeks' time. Accommodation in the city is very hard to obtain.

'We'd like to be settled before the baby arrives at the end of May,' Fiona told us. She went on to explain that Alex is presently working sixteen-hour shifts as a guard (£70 per week) in order to provide for them both. There was no bitterness in her voice, just simple statement of fact. I felt very drawn to them. I can relate more to their circumstances now. We prayed for one another before they had to leave. I felt unexpectedly light-hearted as I cleared away the coffee mugs afterwards. That young couple called at just the right moment - they've really encouraged me.

Tuesday 17 February

Les's farm work has finished. This morning he spent a while writing to the list of agents. He's been collecting details from newspapers, exploring many different avenues.

'I wish I had other skills to offer besides flying!' he's always saying these days.

I noticed he was typing out several copies of the details of his past work and qualifications.

'I know this wretched thing off by heart now!' he grinned, over 'elevenses'.

I packed peanut butter and jam sandwiches into a box and Les drove off to Aberdeen just before midday. He wanted to visit several more agencies in person. He seemed quite cheerful.

'There's a good chance of finding something,' he's told me. 'Even if it's selling screws or driving a delivery van.'

I heard the first oyster-catcher of the season when I cycled to the village this afternoon. How I love their noisy, hectic dash across the sky. I can't think how they manage to keep it up at all hours of the day and night.

Les was home at 6 p.m. 'Feel as if I've walked miles!' he said. 'I went to as many agencies as possible.'

'Much to offer?'

Les frowned. 'Not really, specially when they discovered I wasn't interested in long-term work. Not too interested in my qualifications, either. Most are looking for engineers – anyone with skills to offer the oil industry.'

'Did you tell them you'd be willing to take anything?'

'Yes, but they're not too concerned about labouring work, and such-like. Their income depends on placing people who have specific qualifications.'

'Was it a wasted afternoon, then?'

'No, I wouldn't say that. Several agencies have taken details and asked me to keep in touch. They could come up with something before the end of the month. Might even ask around for me.'

Nothing at all on the flying scene, at present.

Paul and Bob are still doing their best down south.
Les is grateful for their continuing concern.

Wednesday 18 February

The typewriter's been busy again. Les was following
up more ideas gleaned from yesterday's contacts. I
posted eight letters for him at the village this
morning to go by first-class post.

It's Stuart's appointment tomorrow. We plan to
drive in, collect him from school at midday, then
enjoy a picnic lunch together before going to the
hospital.

'What's on your lesson timetable tomorrow
afternoon?' I asked Stuart casually this evening.

'My worst subjects. French, Maths, and Latin.'

'Well, we've got news for you. You can give the
lot a miss!'

His eyes lit up. 'Yes, Mum? How come?'

'The doctor here wants you to see a specialist at
the hospital. Just for a check-up. The appointment is
at two o-clock.'

There was a pause, then, 'Goody, that means
the whole afternoon off!' He didn't ask any further
questions. Just wanted to know about lunch.

'We'll have a picnic. Where would you like to go?'

'Down by the beach, please!'

Thursday 19 February

Everything went as planned this morning. We
watched an angry grey sea flinging itself against the
breakwaters as we sat in the car enjoying our
sandwiches. I had also bought a Mars bar to share
as an after-lunch treat. A small trawler was pushing
its way bravely out from the sheltering harbour,
tossing about as the waves thumped against the hull.

'Glad *I'm* not on board!' Les said.

We were just on time at the hospital. I tried to
read a book while we waited but couldn't concentrate.
The specialist called us in. He repeated the
cardiogram, then asked a few quetions. His
experienced eye glanced down the strip of film.

'That looks fine,' he smiled. 'No obvious problem. I'll be writing to your doctor soon. Excuse me now, I must be off to a meeting.'

'So it's nothing to worry about after all!' I beamed at Les, while Stuart leapt happily off the couch and dived into his shirt. I felt as if I'd suddenly come out into sunshine after groping through a long dark tunnel.

'Well, I don't know about that,' I heard Les say. 'We haven't got the final word yet. We'll have to wait on the specialist's report.'

He's hesitant as usual, trying to balance my cheerful confidence. I could tell he was relieved, though. All of us were light-hearted as we drove home.

'What were the doctors worried about, anyway?' asked Stuart.

'They just wondered why there seemed to be some interruption in your heart-beat rhythm. But it's quite normal again now. Nothing to worry about,' I told him.

Wednesday 25 February

Another week has dragged by. No word from the agencies. Les was feeling low this morning. Unusually silent.

'I'll try phoning round some of the oil companies I wrote to last week,' he decided. 'They should have had time to consider my enquiry by now.' He drew a chair up to telephone, pulled the list from his file and started dialling.

The first isn't recruiting at present. The second only interested in qualified men. The third hasn't had time to process Les's letter yet – the person concerned is off sick. The fourth offered to put application forms into the post, but warned that openings are scarce. The secretary of the fifth stopped to chat for a short while. Told Les that her company is now receiving 300 enquiry letters a week. Most are dealt with by the person who opens mail, getting no further than that. 'No point in referring them to anyone higher up,' the secretary said. 'We haven't any work to offer anyway.'

Les finished the call. Got up and walked over to the kitchen window.

'I think I'll go out and dig over the vegetable patch. We'll need to plant seed potatoes quite soon.'

'April, Margaret said.'

'Oh? A few weeks yet then. Never mind. I'll do some digging anyway. I must find something to keep me occupied, or I'll go crazy.'

He put on an old coat and boots and went to fetch the spade. I watched him as I cleaned the boys' bedroom-window. A lump came to my throat. I couldn't bear to see him turning over the hard brown earth, desperately trying to work out his pent-up frustration. I can hardly believe that only last February he was in command of a passenger airliner. Now he has to dig furrow after furrow of that stubborn plot in order to try and fill the long empty hours. The misery of it all is more painfully real than ever before. And if it's hurting me, what must it be doing to Les?

'I so much need a faith-boost,' he said to me again this morning, as we were washing breakfast dishes together. There was such plaintiveness in his quiet voice. I can't get those words out of my mind. If only there was something positive, however small, to cling to. The breakthrough *must* come soon.

James's wife, Mary, phoned this afternoon.

'How's Les?'

It was hard to answer, particularly as he was right there in the room with me. I've found such conversations more difficult lately. The concern shown by friends is a comfort, yet I'm aware of the need to choose my words carefully.

'Getting on quite well thanks. Still no work yet, though.'

It must have been hard to answer.

'I'm sorry,' she said and I caught the sympathy in those two short words. She asked after Stuart, and

I was glad I could share some good news.

Mary's call reminded me of many others who phone to express their caring. I find I'm hesitating to give details now. Not so much to shield Les (he's willing for news to be shared if its worded in the right way) but rather to spare *them*. I don't want to keep on about our problem. There's a limit to the amount of trouble it's right to offload on to others.

'Shall I walk up to the village and get your shopping?' Les offered later.

'Yes, thanks! That would be a help. I'm nearly out of instant coffee.'

The youngsters were just in from school. Murray was carrying a coat-rack over one shoulder. 'Made it in woodwork classes!' he told me.

'Well done, lad! It will match the pine beams in the hall. Just what we're needing, too. Dad will probably screw it into place tomorrow.'

Les walked in through the back door. 'I got you a really good offer on the coffee!' he smiled. I unpacked the shopping-basket. There was a tin of expensive ground coffee at the bottom.

'Is this it?'

'Yes, the girl said it was down in price, and worth buying!'

I couldn't bear to tell him it's about the most expensive kind going, even at reduced cost. It will take a large bite out of the housekeeping funds this week.

'Oh, that's good!' I said, trying to sound pleased – face hidden as I bent to put it on the lowest shelf of the store cupboard! I shall save it for treats.

Thursday 26 February

Very cold, grey day. I was glad to get back from a quick trip to the village this morning. Les opened the front door before I had time to turn the handle. An unusually happy look on his face!

'I'll put the bike away!' he said. He followed me

into the kitchen. 'I've got some good news at last!'

'Have you!' I beamed. 'What is it?'

'Dyce company phoned, offering me an interview. Turbo-props. They're planning to expand up here.' There was that twinkle in his eyes again. His face was bright with excitement.

'Marvellous!' Was all I could say. Talk about a faith-boost! I wish I could phone round all our friends and tell them.

'And to think that *they* contacted you this time!' I commented, making mid-morning drinks from the instant coffee I'd just bought. 'Couldn't be better!'

'Yes, this time they must have stopped to look through their files before making any crew needs public. I don't think anyone else is in the running yet, either.'

'When's the interview?'

'Not for another three weeks. Senior pilot is going off on holiday tomorrow, but he promised to see me as soon as he returns.'

'Pity you've got to wait.'

'Yes, but I'll need a bit of time anyway, I want to read up as much information as possible on this type of aircraft. Must get my "medical" updated, too. I'll sit and work it all out this morning. Maybe James could lend me one of his engine manuals. He should have the right one for this plane ... '

He's obviously thrilled – ideas spilling out of his mind. I'm so excited for him. A happy contrast to yesterday's despair.

Month 14

Sunday 1 March

We've been here four years now; we moved in on 1 March, 1977.

'It's the longest time we've ever been in one place, isn't it?' Rachel asked, over a late Sunday breakfast. She's right.

Murray had hung a string of peanuts from the overhanging roof outside the kitchen, and as we lingered over cereal and toast we watched a determined bluetit struggling to extract the biggest nut he could find. It took ages, but he didn't give up till he got it out.

'That bird's certainly made his point!' I smiled at Les.

Monday 2 March

Les was deep in that Rolls Royce Dart Engine manual this morning. He's glad to be packing away all the needed information in preparation for the interview. Just over two weeks to go now. This afternoon a doctor at Dyce updated Les's 'medical' in readiness for possible flying soon. Expensive, but essential. Les enjoyed getting the necessary 'red tape' in order.

Tuesday 3 March

Heavy rain today. Large puddles all over the newly-dug vegetable patch. There's a broad carpet of green beneath the beeches now, and reeds thrusting up fresh spikes along the river-bank. Don joined us for lunch. He brought his final-year dissertation which Les has agreed to type. It will be a welcome time-filler while we wait for that interview.

Friday 13 March

We both went to see the doctor about Stuart this morning. He shared with us the specialist's report. Apparently an interruption of impulses between brain and heart caused the November incident. It was still evident on the January cardiograph, but is no longer present. All tests are now normal; no treatment necessary. It could happen again if Stuart were to get a sudden fright – like that choke. In the event of recurrence there's nothing to be done, except turn him on one side. Normal heart function would resume in a few seconds.

'Just one of those things,' the doctor told us. We both felt reassured, though we hope it will prove to have been a one-off crisis. What a relief! My mind's at peace about the lad now. I no longer need to get edgy if he's late in from school, or away at the swimming-pool without me or Les. He hates us checking up on his activities anyway.

'Can't help feeling very grateful to God about that report,' Les said as we walked home.

Saturday 14 March

I walked along the street to Sally's this morning. She was sitting at the kitchen table reading the paper. 'Come in and have a chat!' Typical Sally – she's always got time for people. I admire her for it. All along she's shown real concern for us, too, asking at length about the situation. I find it helpful to talk. Openness is important. I never want people to treat unemployment as a 'no-no' subject with us, for fear they cause embarrassment. Sally's not like that, anyway.

The kitchen clock ticked away. It was time to go

and make our hamburger lunch.

'Wait a minute. I've got something for you!' Sally said, opening the fridge door. Norwegian cheese, brought back by her husband after a recent Scandinavian visit. A real delicacy!

'No, Sally, you mustn't give us any. It's too special!' I objected.

'Yes, I *will*,' she insisted, cutting off a large hunk. 'We must share the good things together, as well as the hard!'

I walked slowly home, thinking of her words. There was real truth there. Something to store away.

Monday 16 March

'The company's senior pilot should be back from holiday today, so I'll probably get a call telling me when to attend that interview on Wednesday,' Les said this morning. He waited all day for the phone message, while busily putting the finishing touches to Don's dissertation.

At 6 p.m. there was still no word.

'Guess they'll contact me tomorrow.'

Tuesday 17 March

I spent the morning at the typewriter. My new book outline is beginning to take shape at last. Les was restless. He can't think why the phone call from Dyce hasn't come through yet. He spent a while with that manual, then sorted out the seed potatoes. He left them spread out on top of the kitchen cupboard 'To sprout a little before I plant them'.

'I don't think I can wait any longer,' Les said to me at midday. 'I shall have to contact the senior pilot myself. I so hoped he'd make the first move. I don't like doing it this way round.' He dialled the number.

'Sorry, he's away on a Shetlands flight at present,' the secretary said. 'I'll ask him to phone when the flight gets back.'

The call came through at 3 p.m. Les was ready with a pen to write down details of the interview time, etc. The man at the other end seemed to be doing most of the talking.

'Yes, I see,' Les said. He put the pen down. 'Yes, I understand.' Something was up. Why weren't they making plans for tomorrow? What had happened? The call continued. Lengthy explanations from the company pilot. Then Les said goodbye and rang off. He sat there for a few seconds, hand still resting on the receiver, the room silent. I didn't dare ask what was up. I couldn't bear the thought of what might be coming. Les turned to me, his face pale, serious.

'Well, that's a bit of a disappointment,' he said at last. 'They're not offering me an interview after all.'

Oh *no*! Not after all the eager anticipation of the past three weeks, the probability of flying work at last. Isn't this our breakthrough? It *must* be. I wanted to rush over to Les and take this bitter disappointment from him, so he wouldn't have to endure the agony of another 'no'. But there was nothing I could do. Nothing at all. Except to say again those all-too-frequent words – 'I'm sorry!'

'So am I,' Les answered, masking his shock behind a quick smile.

'But why this sudden change? It doesn't make sense to me.'

'Apparently there are company changes afoot at head office. Until the senior pilot up here knows more he isn't in a position to recruit personnel or even offer interviews. So he's stalling for a while. He'll let me know more within the next few days.'

'So it isn't a final "no" then?'

'Not at the moment. But I don't think I should count on anything now.'

There was a deep sadness in his voice. We sat together in silence for a while, seeing shafts of spring sunlight playing on the still-bare branches of the trees. I thought of the eagerness with which Les updated his 'medical', the long hours gladly spent studying that engine manual. I saw again the happy anticipation on his face, so suddenly absent now. If only the senior pilot knew how much Les has counted on the prospect of an interview ...

Perhaps he does know. But what difference can it make? He's unwillingly caught up in this growing employment tangle, too – a tangle which inevitably ousts practical concern. It has to. One man's needs can't be considered and met when those of the whole group press even more heavily. It's a wretched predicament, particularly for those in authority.

Today's local paper has a front page paragraph headed '350 to be laid off at paper mill.' Many of these are in their forties and fifties, having spent several years with the firm.

'Remember George?' I said to Les. 'He's on the senior management staff there, isn't he? How awful for him to have to do something like that.'

'Yes, I'm glad I'm not in his shoes,' Les answered.

The hopelessness of it all is overwhelming. Nothing can be done. There's no way to ease the distress, the pain, the gnawing anxiety of redundancy. It's all so final.

The late post brought a parcel. Six copies of the book I finished last summer. So it's out! How strange that they should come today, just when I was feeling particularly low. I was glad to see those small books. They brought a welcome touch of pleasure, but I hesitated to open the cover of the top copy. I decided I'd wait till no one was around.

Wednesday 18 March
Our usual Wednesday morning Bible discussion group at the Church hall today. We've been looking at the Ten Commandments – finding they're very much up-to-date. I hurried home to get lunch, hoping to catch up on some writing. Les was reading a magazine. The hours are dragging, now that there's not much point in studying that manual.

Perhaps we could go out for a picnic lunch together? The writing could wait. Les was keen on the idea. He packed sandwiches, while I heated soup. We bought a chocolate bar on our way through the village – it added a special touch to the occasion!

'Let's go up the Lord's Throat road!' I suggested.
(It follows the Don upstream.) The river is running
high at present, foaming around each boulder with an
impressive show of spring force. Les parked
overlooking larch plantations and ploughed fields,
with Cairn William just beyond. Magnificent setting
for our cheese sandwiches! A strong wind chased a
few stray snowflakes in an attempt to oust the sun.
We watched the changing pattern of grey shadows
and golden light as we ate. There was time for a
walk along the forest path before returning home.
Trees murmured to the wind, and a couple of burns
tumbled and gurgled on their way down towards the
Don. The pine-scented air was keen and cold. On the
drive back we noticed some bullocks trying to graze a
bare brown field. The new grass shoots were taking
their time.

'It's funny how spring dawdles up here, isn't it!' I
commented to Les. I think he enjoyed the break. It's
important to give him plenty of undivided time at
present. So easy to get on with my own 'thing' and
forget how long each empty day must seem.

Wednesday 25 March
This morning's Bible discussion found us tossing out
views on God's discipline, following on from all those
'Thou shalt nots' of the Ten Commandments. We
came to the conclusion that if God is completely right
and trustworthy, then the way he disciplines us must
be, too. That's easy to say in a cool moment; hard to
accept when we're in the thick of an uncomfortable
experience. On my way home I found myself relating
the same truth of God's 'rightness' to our own
situation at present. I don't think it's a 'discipline' in
the negative sense, but it *is* proving to be a
schooling. A very painful and exacting schooling. Yet
if God's 'rightness' has allowed it, that is also our
refuge. He's permitting it only so that we might
ultimately benefit from it. Again, so easily said, yet
so hard to accept when everything inside me wants
to scream out in protest at the pain of such a trial for
Les.

Over lunch Les said, 'You know the car's MOT certificate expires on 7th April?'

'Yes?'

'Well, I regret to inform you that its funeral is now due to take place on that date.'

'What do you mean?'

'I took it to the garage for a once-over this morning. The rust is so extensive that the cost of welding work would be prohibitive, and it would only delay the inevitable.'

'So it's "goodbye"?'

'Yes.' Les had seen this coming. Even so, it's a blow.

I tried to find some positive advantage.

'It's obviously going to be hard,' I began, 'but summer's on the way now, which means we can get around quite easily on bikes. We could cycle to Inverurie together for the supermarket groceries once a week, and there are always buses to Aberdeen. It will be a relief not to have licence and insurance costs, or petrol bills ...'

Les listened in silence. He can't look at it that way. The car means more to him than I realized. As important in its own way as that first motorbike he owned nearly thirty years ago.

'I hope it won't be long before we can buy another vehicle,' Les said slowly.

Sunshine beckoned us out this afternoon. We cycled past the golf course, enjoying the scattering of purple and gold crocuses beneath the roadside trees. Les free-wheeled, watching a particularly impressive drive by one golfer. 'Good shot!' I commented. I hope Les will be able to resume playing soon. I can see he's yearning to be out on that green!

Friday 27 March

Off to a city supermarket this morning, glad of a chance to stock the larder with basics before the car goes. The shelves are now groaning under the weight of all those tins! We had a picnic lunch on the sea front – everything gleaming in the sunlight, tide far out, sand smooth and gold. The harbour pilot boat was busy escorting oil-rig supply vessels to quayside berths.

We stopped in the village to collect *Flight* on the way home. Ailie called 'Hallo!' I was glad to see her. News of Neil's self-employment project is good. It's going ahead well now, despite earlier snags.

'That's great!' Les said to Ailie. 'Tell Neil how pleased we are, won't you?'

Flight advert columns were disappointing. No jobs for fixed-wing pilots.

'I could easily get something if I could fly a helicopter,' Les said. Friends have often asked why he doesn't try this line. But the cost of training is prohibitive, and his age stands against him now. 'Anyway, I'd hate to fly one of those noisy machines!' Les always tells them.

Monday 30 March

Hot today – and it's still only March. Les was outside in his shirt sleeves tidying climbing rose bushes this afternoon. A British Airways Trident came in overhead.

'That'll be Bernice's plane,' I called out.

Les drove to Dyce to meet his sister. So glad she can stop-over with us en route from Malaysia to Canada!

We walked along the river-bank together after tea. It was good to show Bernice our Aberdeenshire surroundings. She told us about life in a busy, bustling Far Eastern city.

'Recently a Malaysian man set up "house" beneath a bush opposite our office,' she said. 'We used to watch him every day. He obviously hadn't got work, so he filled the hours by keeping his bush area tidy, and as homely as possible. He even swept the dirt "floor" several times a day. It was sad to see, yet I couldn't help admiring that fellow. Never seemed to lose his self-respect.'

We walked on towards the bridge. Bernice's story stayed in my mind. It seems that everyone is geared to work, even if it's only keeping a bush home neat and clean.

Month 15

Wednesday 1 April

The children didn't seem to have remembered about
April Fool's Day – so I didn't bother to remind them!

It was sad to see Bernice go. Les drove her across
to visit the Pitlochry aunts this morning, before she
catches the London train later this week.

This evening I walked to the usual study prayer
group. There were four others present – all men. One
had chosen 'work' as the study topic for tonight. I sat
back and listened, glad of a chance to hear other men
putting forward their views on employment. My mind
kept turning to a quote seen recently in a magazine –
people in a small isolated USA village maintaining
that 'work is a virtue, welfare a disgrace'. Did these
men feel the same? (All have good, apparently secure
jobs.) They all agreed that work is a God-given thing;
people are programmed that way. (I thought of the
Malaysian man.) Then the subject of unemployment
crept in.

'Welfare's not a disgrace. But it's open to abuse
by some.' 'It can take the keen edge off initiative too!'

Their discussion grew more intense. They'd never
experienced unemployment. Everything was so cut
and dried. I felt tears pricking my eyes. I blinked
them back quickly – mustn't let them see my dismay.

'But you don't understand,' I wanted to say. 'You
talk so easily about such hard things ...'

I held the words back. The group had been pressing on a tender spot, but they weren't to know.

Friday 3 April

'Fantastic! School's over for a whole two and a half weeks!' the boys cried, sparring with each other in delight this evening.

'Oh, groan!' Les said, putting on a deep sigh of despair.

'You miserable old spoil-sport, Dad!' Rachel objected, jumping on him from behind and forcing Les to recant.

'Tell you what,' he said, 'All three of you can start work straight away by helping me to plant tatties in the garden.'

It was fun to watch them getting tangled in the line Les was using to mark each row. Murray and Rachel gave up and fetched rackets for a badminton game on the grass beside the river. It was hopeless! A mischievous wind kept snatching away the shuttlecock.

E. arrived with her portable TV set. 'Just thought you'd enjoy looking after this for the next fortnight while I'm away,' she explained.

Whoops of delight from the three youngsters. They hardly stopped to say 'thank you'. The set was soon installed in the boys' bedroom.

'Now we can watch all those smashing programmes over Easter – the space shuttle too!' Stuart beamed.

'Yes, and the Eurovision Song Contest tomorrow night,' added Rachel.

It looks like we're in for some enjoyment ahead. I don't think Les will need to groan too often.

Saturday 4 April

Les gave the car its last wash-and-brush-up this morning.

'It looks quite reasonable on the outside,' he said, stepping back and trying to picture that smart white Ford we bought just two years ago from a dealer. 'I'm

sure someone will want it!' He's decided to try selling
the vehicle. An advert in the local paper has already
brought some enquiries.

The postman arrived while we were smartening
up the car. One letter. It was from the Christian
bookshop in town, explaining that an anonymous
donor has deposited £50 credit for us. What
thoughtfulness! I slowly re-read the letter, taking in
the excitement of it all.

'To think we can buy £50-worth of books!' I
smiled.

'Yes, that's going to be a treat,' Les said. 'But I
can't help feeling reluctant to accept. It's that same
feeling all over again.'

'I know what you mean.'

Like the battery incident, we haven't any choice,
though. This generous and unusual gift must simply
be accepted with gratitude, too. The donor would
want it that way.

This evening I remembered one or two good
books we've seen reviewed recently. I listed them,
ready for our next visit to Aberdeen.

Sunday 5 April

'Dad, when's the car going?' Stuart asked as we
walked over the hill to church.

'Hope to sell it by Tuesday, the MOT runs out
then.' We all walked on in silence for a while.

'When will you get another?'

'Don't know. Soon I hope.'

'What will it be? Something exciting like a Golf
GTI?' The lad's face lit up at the mere thought of
owning such a vehicle.

'W-e-l-l,' Les said.

'Yes, let's get one of those!' Murray was all agog,
too, now. They've both been studying a friend's
glossy motoring magazine this week.

'We'll see!' was all they could extract from Dad.
The twins interpreted this as a promise that the next
car won't be another ordinary Ford.

'How about a Renault?' suggested Rachel.

'They're nice!'

'No, a Golf GTI would be *much* better!' Stuart insisted.

We were at the churchyard gate by now. I bet those boys spent the next hour dreaming of the day when they'd boast of 'My Dad's fantastic new turbo! Goes 120 miles an hour. 143 horse-power, of course!'

This afternoon we set off to Stonehaven for our last family outing in the car. It was misty at the coast, but not too cold. The harbour was quiet and empty. There was a launch towing a water-skier just beyond the harbour wall.

'Wish we could have a go!' said Stuart.

'What's the time?' asked Murray. 'We just *must* get home in time to see the Muppet Show!'

Monday 6 April
Senior pilot from that Dyce company phoned this morning. Over a fortnight since Les was last in touch. He's been waiting eagerly for this call.

'Regret to say we are not going to be able to offer you an interview after all.'

'Not really a surprise,' Les commented afterwards. 'But a big disappointment all the same.'

He got out the employment file and started looking through the contents. This final 'no' had brought painful facts into sharp focus again. There are no work openings of any kind yet — aviation or otherwise — despite continuing enquiries, and contacts with agencies. Yet, for all that he feels he must *do* something. He can't bear the thought of continuing on unemployment benefit much longer. The quarterly bills are due again now. '*Must* find work. Anything, anywhere - just to be able to provide adequately for the family again, and to occupy the long, empty hours.'

This morning the temptation to give up was sudden and strong. What's the point in hoping for an aviation breakthrough? It always comes to nothing. Why bother to get the 'medical' updated? Why spend hours keeping informed about aircraft engines? It's

useless. It only serves to feed that desperate urge to
fly once more. Better to try and smother the urge. It's
not likely to be satisfied now. For the time being he'll
go all out to find something along another avenue.

Stuart cycled to the village and bought Dad a
local newspaper. He's aware of the disappointment,
and eager to try to help. Les used to skim over large
chunks of the 'Situations Vacant' page. Now he
examines each advert carefully.

'I think I'll try these two,' he told me, pointing
out an oil company and a helicopter operation, both
needing handling staff, 'as well as sending off for
details about some of the job ideas I've collected in
my file.'

He fetched the typewriter and began. A sadness
has settled over the house today. I think we all
realize that the odds are being steadily stacked
higher and higher against us. Les is fighting another
battle with those persistent boils, too. 'But I won't go
and see the doctor,' he insists. 'I much prefer your
special ointment.'

Rachel phoned a friend for a long chat about
nothing in particular – or so it seemed to us.

'You'd better ring off now,' Les called, after about
eight minutes. She glared, then suddenly softened.

'I'll pay,' she told us. 'But mind you, I'm not the
worst one for making long phone calls.' We all knew
that dig was aimed at Dad.

She got a large sheet of paper and stuck it up
near the telephone. Each family member has his/her
own column.

'Now, whenever someone makes a call they've got to
mark it down,' Rachel instructed. 'Then we'll add up
each column at the end of the month and see who's got
the most.'

'Good idea,' said Les. 'Anything to make you
more careful about phoning friends!'

Tuesday 7 April
Happy sight — lambs gambolling in the fields across
the river!

Les has been busy writing more enquiry letters.
He's also run off several copies of his job details. I
saw him glancing through the Airline Directory
again last night. He's writing to six of them – in
various parts of the world – 'just in case they've got
something going, after all.'

He tried the job centre in Aberdeen. There was a
helpful lady on the other end of the phone. 'Wish I
had more to offer you, though.' She must be always
saying that these days. Then, 'Did you mention you'd
be willing to take *anything*?'

'Yes.'

'Well, there are a couple of short-term jobs here.
Rather unusual. The first is working at the top of
high scaffolding in the city. Any good?'

'No, I'd only consider that if I'd had scaffolding
experience. It's rather risky otherwise.'

'Well, how about this? We're needing someone to
design costumes and direct a play for young people
at a centre in the town. Do you fancy that?'

'Sorry, but that's just not my scene at all.
Wouldn't know where to start.'

Poor Les. It's true, he *is* willing to take anything,
but there are limits! I hope that helpful lady hasn't
labelled him 'unco-operative'.

Murray took a friend downriver in the dinghy
this afternoon. They had great fun huffing and
puffing as they blew the thing up.

'The rapids were magic fun!' both reported as
they stood dripping on the kitchen mat. Shivering,
too – it may be April but there's still a sharp nip in
the air.

After tea we sprawled over the beds in the boys'
room to see a double bill of 'Tom and Jerry'. It was
hilarious. We laughed so much we almost made
ourselves sick. It was so good to hear Les guffawing
away, as loudly as the rest.

A beautiful calm night. Murray and his friend
pitched a tent beyond the back fence and I took them
cocoa and biscuits. The river scene was silver in the

faint moonlight.

'Let's go for a walk!' I suggested to Les. We don't usually do such things at nearly midnight. But I couldn't resist it this time. We strolled along the river-bank, seeing the shaft of light from the quarter-moon being broken into a thousand shimmering fragments by the tumbling water. A moment to store in my memory.

Thursday 9 April

We sold the car at last today (£60). The man seemed pleased with it, though he knew all about the rust. He works in a garage nearby and can weld the chassis himself. It was sad to see our Cortina leave without us and disappear round the nearby bend.

Later Les and I cycled to Inverurie for groceries – the first time I've made the trip. There was so much to enjoy en route this warm, sunny day – an early clump of shy violets, budding celandines, wild daffodils. We heard a song thrush, too. Marvellous feel of air through my hair as we sped down the last long hill into the town.

'Do you think we're breaking the 30-mile per hour speed limit?' I called back to Les. The whole trip went well. It took us twenty-five minutes each way. There was a happy sense of satisfaction as we reached home with bike-baskets loaded. The larder shelves are quite well stocked again now.

Thursday 16 April

'We're cycling to Inverurie swimming-pool this afternoon!' Stuart announced at lunch-time. 'Cameron's coming, too.' They seemed to be gone ages. At almost supper-time they were still not back. Murray arrived at 6 p.m., pushing his bike.

'What's happened?'

'When we got out of the swimming-pool my cycle tyres were flat. Someone had let the air out and pinched the valves.'

'What did you do?'

'Thought I'd walk home, but then Cameron

decided to phone his Mum and tell her. He said he
knew she'd be willing to come and collect me in the
car.'

'Did she?'

'Yes, and she brought my bike back, too.'

'Wasn't that good of her!' I commented to Les.
'But it makes me feel embarrassed. Cameron must
know we haven't a car now; that's why he asked his
mother to help.' Our feelings are very mixed over
incidents like this. We value the kindness shown, but
hate to involve friends in any way.

'Where are Stuart and Cameron?'

'At Cameron's house.'

The phone rang. It was Stuart. 'Can I stay to
supper here? Cameron's mother has invited me, and
it smells delicious!'

Wasn't that good of her? It was quite enough to
help Murray out of a tight spot, without including
Stuart in a family meal as well. It reminded me of all
the other times when friends round about have gone
out of their way to 'special' our three over recent
months – a day at the Black's farm, a trip to the
seaside fun-fair, an evening at the cinema. It means
a lot to all five of us!

It was quiet at home here this evening. Stuart
was still out; Murray trying to fly his kite from the
river-bank; Rachel babysitting next door. It gave me
a chance to talk with Les. There's not much
opportunity to do so, at present, with the youngsters
here all day. There's nothing further on the job scene.
One or two replies from foreign airlines. No openings.
'What about those two companies needing handling
staff?' I asked.

'Positions filled.'

I know Les finds it hard to have to report all these
negative responses to me, yet at the same time he
needs to off-load.

'I just don't know what to do next,' he sighed,
leaning back against the settee and shutting his
eyes. 'Where else can I try? What else can I do?'

He knows I haven't an answer. It's a way of

voicing the intense frustration he now feels.

'I don't know how much longer I can go on like this. It's getting to a point where ...'

'I understand. At least, I understand as much as I can.'

The ice-cream van hooted loudly outside. A passing dog snapped at the crouched cat beside our front doorstep. Children skipped happily on the pavement. Two more were plodding along with stilts. Everything around us was carrying on in a normal, ordinary, usually happy pattern. If only life was still normal and ordinary and happy in this house.

'Boredom is the hardest part,' Les continued slowly. 'Not having work to do has thrown me right out of gear. Everything seems wrong. There's nothing to wake up to each morning, nothing to look back on at night. Just an empty, pointless blank.'

'Do you mind me offering your assistance in various ways – like painting the new cupboards at the church hall, or helping to clear all that building rubble up there?'

'No, I'm glad to do anything I can. It helps to pass the long hours.'

He sat deep in thought for a while. Then, 'There's something else which concerns me even more than the boredom.'

'What?'

'I'm losing my sense of direction in all this. I don't know where I'm going now. Thought I did once, but then those promising aviation openings all folded up, leaving me confused. I've tried other possibilities, and they've come to nothing, too. So what next? Where to try? I feel as if I'm going round in tighter and tighter circles. One of these days I'm going to keel over completely.'

I tried to comfort Les, but each word or touch seems so tiny a thing against his overwhelming need.

He straightened up. 'I guess there's nothing for it but to keep on trying, even if I don't know where I'm going,' he told himself in a firm, no-nonsense sort of way. He hates me to glimpse the turmoil underneath.

'That's easy to say, but hard to do,' I commented.

'Yes, I haven't much heart for it,' Les said. 'I find I need real will-power now to pick up the phone or visit those agencies. I have to grit my teeth and force myself into it, especially as most of the contacts are likely to meet with another "no".'

He got up to let the cat in. That passing dog had left her all fluffed up and affronted. Murray strolled in through the back door, dragging yards of tangled kite string. 'Got in a bit of a mess!' Stuart arrived home on his bike. 'You should have seen the size of those chops!' he told us, licking his lips. We packed them off to bed. It was time we turned in, too. It's odd how emotional trauma can make you feel physically spent.

'Do you think you'll sleep tonight?' I asked Les.

'Yes, I never have trouble doing that.'

But my mind was still in top gear. It took a while to slow down. My thoughts turned to Annette. 'It's Thursday. She'll have been at the Inverurie workshop.' Three months since we last saw her. She will be wondering why we haven't been in touch to suggest another lunch-date here. That's not possible now, without the car. I can't explain this to Annette, though. I've hardly told anyone about the car. It seems to accentuate our situation too sharply. Most – though not Annette – will notice in time. I'm finding it hard to find the right words when the situation does have to be explained. Usually I just say, 'We're not mobile at present.' That sounds much better than, 'We don't have a car now.' My last thoughts, as I dropped off to sleep, turned to God. I tried to tell him how desperate I feel on Les's behalf (though God knows already). 'Please show us a way out of all this soon,' I found myself asking. 'Or if not, keep Les from keeling right over. Keep us both holding on to you. Keep trust real ...'

Easter Sunday 19 April

A dull, chilly morning with an odd snatch of

sunshine. The youngsters were eager to rush downstairs and discover Easter eggs beside their breakfast places. I hoped they wouldn't mind the simple – yet delicious! – eggs I bought for them this time.

'Yippee, "Caramac" eggs!' yelled Stuart. 'You know we like those best don't you, Mum?'

Rachel walked in, hands behind her back. She slipped a large package on to my plate. The three of them stood back, waiting for my reaction.

'Hey, what's this?'

'Your egg, Mum!'

'But it's huge!'

'Yes, the largest, poshest one we could find!'

'Don't forget you've got to share it with Dad,' Murray added.

I smiled to myself. There's me choosing smaller eggs this year, hoping the three of them won't mind, while they club together and really splurge on *us*.

'Remember last Easter?' said Rachel.

'Oh, yes!' butted in Stuart. 'And going along those Amsterdam canals in a river-boat!'

'Pizzas for lunch, too,' added Murray.

It brought back memories. How much has happened since then.

I heard my first 1981 skylark as I cycled to kirk for 9.30 a.m. communion. Such a jubilant sound. Just right for Easter Sunday. House martins were skimming low over the fields, full of 'I've arrived!' enthusiasm. Everything's alive and excited this weekend. I feel cross with myself for not entering fully into the joy of it all. This Easter doesn't seem like most I've known. Inner heaviness keeps me from responding to the thrill of it all. My mind even wandered during those loud, stirring hymns with all their 'Alleluias'. Yet surely Jesus understands. When he rose from death he didn't suddenly cut himself off from all suffering. He feels with us – with me – still. The thought's a comfort.

Lin and Trevor and the boys called in
unexpectedly this evening.

'For you!' Lin smiled, handing me a bouquet of
daffodils from her garden. Their delicate fragrance
spelt 'spring'. The boys brought two tiny wild rabbits
out of their pockets. 'Easter bunnies to show you!'

'Oh, aren't they gorgeous!' Rachel cried. 'So tame,
too.'

'The mother abandoned them when our dog
found the warren,' Trevor explained.

'I don't think they'll last long, though. It's very
hard to rear wild rabbits.'

The evening was damp and cold. We relaxed
around the fireside once the family had gone. Les put
on the 'Messiah' record. Such majestic music!

'Worthy is the Lamb that was slain!'

Thursday 23 April

Lunch-time news gave the latest unemployment
figures. One in ten out of work in Britain. More than
2½ million looking for jobs.

It was warm enough outside to sit on the garden
bench for after-lunch coffee. Peaceful now, with the
youngsters back at school!

'I've had an idea!' Les said. 'I think I'll make
enquiries about those TOPS (Training Opportunities
Scheme) courses, and see if I can get some admin.
training. Then I could look for ground work with one
of the Dyce airlines. That way I also could keep in
touch with latest flying possibilities.'

'Sounds a good plan! Could be quite interesting.'

I was glad to see Les's sudden enthusiasm. It looked
a hopeful possibility.

Les had a lengthy phone chat with the advisor at
the Professional and Executive Recruitment Office.

'What's the score?' I asked when he rejoined me
in the garden.

'Nil, I'm afraid. I felt sorry for the man. It
sounded as if he spends all day telling enquirers the
same story. Most TOPS courses here have been axed.

Those for off-shore engineers are continuing. Several members of the advisory staff have gone too, so I can't even ask someone for alternative advice.'

'Extraordinary situation, isn't it?' I commented. 'With so much redundancy, TOPS courses would seem to be in urgent demand, yet try to enrol and you find most have been discontinued. Can't win, can you!'

'Oh well, that's that, I suppose,' said Les. 'Time I planted those carrot seeds. Were you wanting spinach put in, too?'

'Yes, please.'

'Can't think why. It's disgusting stuff!'

Beef olives for supper tonight. The youngsters were pleased. It makes a pleasant treat to welcome them home with. As I served the casserole I realized that one big 'plus' of living more simply is the fact that ordinary things are suddenly raised to 'treat' level. And why not? Menu items like beef, 'buttries' or rice cereal are enjoyed all the more because they're infrequent and therefore special. It's the same with a bus outing or a film evening – even twice-weekly bath nights! They're looked forward to.

After the meal we read some verses from Matthew's Gospel, Chapter 6 together.

'Do not store up riches for yourselves here on earth ... instead store up riches in heaven ... for your heart will always be where your riches are.'

'That must mean that if we belong to Jesus, and he belongs to us, we're very rich indeed!' Les commented to the youngsters. 'Even if we don't own a Golf GTI!'

Month 16

Saturday 2 May

Les was helping E. move house this morning – her new home's half a mile away. He was glad of something to do. He hopes to dig her new garden next week. The hedge and rose bushes are already transplanted – and surviving, Les hopes.

Sunday 3 May

Great excitement along the river-bank this afternoon – the annual Raft Race. Murray helped crew one youth group craft; Les assisted on the other. Rachel and Stuart joined the shore party and supplied lunch en route by dropping sandwiches down from the footbridge. Their aim was fairly good! It took just over two hours to paddle the seven-mile course and they overtook thirty other rafts on the way down – some literally 'on the way down'! Traffic jams and happy crowds at the finishing line. And a mingled smell of hamburgers and damp clothes. Everyone was feeling festive despite the drizzle.

'Guess who fell in?' grinned Les, when we located our teams at last.

'I enjoyed my fish's eye-view of the countryside!'

'One of the raft crews caught a salmon!' Stuart told us.

'How? They didn't have a rod on board, surely?'

'No, the craft got submerged by those rapids and

when it came up again there was a salmon on the deck!' It sounded unlikely, but the lads assured us it wasn't just a fishy story.

Everyone was ravenous this evening and the large high tea much appreciated.

Monday 4 May

A letter arrived from the diving equipment company, in Aberdeen. They'd processed Les's recent application for a van-driver's position and wanted him to attend an interview on Wednesday.

'That's great!' I said.

Les's expression was unchanged. 'Don't get too excited. It may come to nothing.'

I stood over the washing-machine while a tangle of sheets churned round and round. It was odd to feel so pleased about the possibility of a driving job. This time last year I wouldn't have wanted Les even to apply for such work. It shows how things have changed. I wanted to tell all our friends that he's been offered an interview at last. Do the neighbours wonder why Les is *still* out of work? It must seem as if we're not trying hard enough, or he's too choosy. Does it look as if we're abusing the welfare system? If only I could explain. But that's not possible.

But for everyone who misunderstands, there are dozens more who show genuine concern. Two weeks ago we had another example. Mrs T. came across with a delicious chicken casserole. 'I made too much for our family,' she explained as she handed me a large covered dish. 'So here's enough for you, too!' She hesitated at the front door. 'You do understand, don't you? It's a gift, not charity.'

'Yes, of course I understand,' I tried to assure her. 'And we appreciate your thoughtfulness very much. Just wait till those lads see our chicken supper!'

Wednesday 6 May

Les took the midday bus to Aberdeen. I did so hope the interview would go well. He returned with Stuart on the 6 p.m. bus. I met them at the door. 'Any news?'

'Not yet. They'll be writing. Might take time.
There were twenty-five of us after two positions. One
driving, one in the stores department. Guess how
many applicants altogether?'

'Fifty or so?'

'Four hundred and fifty!'

'What? They must have been swamped. It speaks
well for you, though, being selected from so many.'

'Well, the final selection is all that's going to
matter.'

Thursday 7 May

Rachel was home today, supposed to be studying for
'higher grade' geography tomorrow. But I couldn't
blame her for being distracted when Sandra brought
over a fat mail-order catalogue.

'I'm due for my coffee-break now, anyway,'
Rachel told me, stretching out on the floor to browse
through all those pages of fashion clothes. I saw her
making a long list of planned purchases. There's
something sad about such eager not-to-be-realized
pleasure.

Murray pounced on the catalogue as soon as he
got in this afternoon. After a while he went and
fetched his savings.

'Look how much I've got, Dad!' he called,
spreading the lot out over the carpet. 'Soon be richer
than you!'

Les paused in the doorway (just in from digging
E's garden). 'Cheeky little monkey!'

Stuart arrived home, saw twenty-five pound notes
on the floor. 'I've got more than that!' he bragged.
'And we're due another pound tomorrow aren't we,
Mum?' (Friday's pocket-money day.)

He dumped his school-bags on the armchair, then
stood still for a few moments, thinking hard.

'Dad, you can cut our money down to fifty pence
a week now, if you like.'

'No lad, I'm not going to do that.'

I changed the subject. I don't want the

youngsters to become too money-conscious.

'Where did you get that mysterious-looking brown bag from, Les?'

'Oh, Mrs Johnson saw me digging the garden and brought it out. I think there's some home-made jam inside.'

The bag was heavy. Six jars! One strawberry, two blackcurrant, two redcurrant, and one rhubarb.

'Isn't that kind of her!' I smiled. 'Not one jar, but half a dozen – and just when we've run out.' I must remember to phone Mrs Johnson and tell her how much her gift means.

Friday 8 May

Warm dry weather continues. We're beginning to take the brilliant early morning sunshine for granted. We'll feel cheated when the rain returns. Our Dutch tulip bulbs are now in full scarlet bloom beside the garden path, and creased leaves are unfolding on the river-side trees. The local cats are glad of the camouflage as they stalk the bluetits in the hawthorns.

Les has been mulling over Paul's latest suggestion. An American group interested in buying a Dakota from Britain would need someone to ferry the aircraft across this summer. Nothing definite yet.

'I'd be keen to do it,' Les told me. 'Could visit the relatives in Canada too, perhaps, and see if there's any flying work going up there.'

Today's *Flight* is advertising a Middle East position. Two months out, one month home.

'Worth trying,' Les said, and phoned the London office for more information. A senior pilot will be leaving for the Middle East next week, taking details of the applicants with him. Les wrote off immediately, hoping to make contact before he left.

After lunch we sat down to read and pray together. We've reached the last chapter of John's Gospel.

'It's interesting how Jesus gave such clear instructions about where those disciples should cast their fishing-net,' Les commented. 'After they'd been trying hard all night without success.'

When he prayed, Les asked, 'Show us where to cast our "net" Lord.' The bewilderment is still there. If only we knew what direction to go in.

This evening the last deep pink bloom dropped from the sitting-room azalea. Eight months of flowers!

Sunday 10 May
A beautiful day. The river level is so low that Old Nog now paddles boldly across the current, almost from bank to bank. I've never seen him do that before.

There were two more new faces at this afternoon's youth group. I'm finding this weekly afternoon session with the youngsters refreshing. They're fun, and they're keen. It takes me right out of myself. Problems recede for a while. It's important to keep busy with other activities – easy to get so wound up in our own concerns that I no longer share with others in *their* interests.

Les was quiet this evening. Deep in thought. 'Pray for me,' he said at bedtime. 'I don't know how I'm going to face another long week of doing nothing.'

His words touched that deep inner spot which is so tender now. It hurts, but the hurt is for him, not myself.

'How much longer has he got to go through this, Lord? I can't bear to see what it's doing to him.'

Wednesday 13 May
Les is glad to be helping with the local Christian Aid shop this week. I spent a while browsing through the goods this afternoon. I found two shirts for the lads, and a smart cardigan for myself. Les tried on a suit. The trousers were worn in parts, but the jacket looked tailor-made. The helpful lady at the stall let him buy

it separately. Rachel came to hunt for bargains on her way home from school. She found an attractive skirt, a bright silk scarf caught her eye, too. All five of us are pleased with the new additions to our summer wardrobes.

A friend insisted on taking a list of grocery items, then buying them for me on her regular visit to the cut-price supermarket. Such a help!

Monday 18 May

'Must *do* something about our situation today,' Les said to me, once the youngsters had left for school. 'I've got to get a clear-cut answer from those local airlines. I keep trying to find out if they need crews for the summer.'

He phoned round. Nothing. 'We'll continue to keep your application on file,' they said.

He tried London for news on that Middle East possibility.

'We're putting a letter in today's post,' is all they would say.

He bought the local paper. No suitable jobs going.

'I feel utterly useless,' Les sighed at the end of a fruitless morning. 'It's this awful realization that no one wants you or needs you any more. You just don't matter.'

This afternoon we walked along the river-bank for a while, seeing the leaves of a lone poplar trembling in the faint breeze. No swans in sight – they must still be nesting. A trout leapt at a hovering fly. The water was clear and shallow now.

Les's words keep going through my mind. He so much needs to be needed. My frustration at not being able to bring him relief was intense. We can't go on like this much longer. Hope is fast running out, trust almost impossible to maintain as doors slam shut against us.

'It's not just the need for bodily activity,' Les told me, as we reached a calmer stretch upriver. My mind

needs to be occupied as well. Mental inactivity throws
me open to all kinds of miserable pressures –
bitterness, despair, depression. And they're so
powerful. I find I'm running out of will-power to fight
back.

We took the stony track past the farm house and
then alongside a small field. Barley shoots were
several inches high, but the surrounding soil dry and
crumbling.

'I think the bitterness is worst of all,' Les
continued. 'Bitterness against circumstances, and
ultimately against God himself. Why doesn't he
intervene? The delay isn't making sense. It seems all
wrong. Yet God can't be wrong, can he?'

We walked on in silence for a while.

'The rightness of God *can* be a refuge for us,
though, can't it?' I asked.

'But not until I've let go of most of the questions!'
Les said.

'God doesn't mind those. He's not shocked or
affronted. Surely he understands our urge to ask
them?'

'Yes, even if he doesn't answer.'

We started back for home, taking the path
through the housing estate. The gardens are bright
with colour, lupins everywhere and early roses heavy
with bloom. Keen gardeners were bedding out
annuals in neat rows. There was a jungle of rhubarb
in one garden, leaves as large as elephant ears.

'Why doesn't he answer our questions, specially
when they're quite legitimate?' I asked.

'Maybe our understanding is too limited. We
couldn't take it all in. But I wish he'd give me a small
clue, a part of an answer, to keep me going.'

'Do you think God's wanting us to keep on
trusting, rather than ask for answers?'

'Yes, I suppose so. But it's almost impossible
sometimes.'

'Maybe knowing that this problem *is* going to end
helps revive trust when it seems to be fading out?'

'Maybe'.

It's hard for Les to be open to any such 'revival' when he's feeling so low.

I remembered words from a friend's recent letter: 'We're praying for Les, for whom this must be a searing experience. But God does not permit testing beyond the point of his children being able to bear it, and be all the stronger and better for it.' That reminded me again of Mary Craig's book *Blessings*, and her insistence that adversity can become creative. It still holds true, but I can't yet see much value in this situation.

Tuesday 19 May

A letter arrived from London. They regret they cannot consider Les's application for the Middle East position.

'Maybe I'll try that other company down south,' Les sighed. 'They're hoping to start operations up here soon.'

He phoned the chief pilot. No immediate likelihood of work. There are 720 applicants on their files.

Wendy rang this evening. Simon is having a few ups and downs, but he's still at school and cheerful as ever. She asked about Les.

'Keep fighting every inch of the way. Never give in. It spells disaster!' There was fellow-feeling in her voice.

Sunday 24 May

Sue stopped me after church today.

'I hesitate to ask. But has Les got work yet?'

'No. Afraid not. He keeps trying every possible avenue, though.'

'Oh, I'm sorry. He looks so cheerful, I thought he must have found something.'

Her genuine concern is a comfort to me in my state of emotional exhaustion. I feel completely drained - like a toothpaste tube, squeezed right out and left all crumpled and crushed.

I appreciated Sue's enquiry, too. I never want

people to feel too embarrassed to ask after our situation. As we walked home I shared Sue's comment with Les.

'You always look so cheerful, she said!'

'It's a mask.'

Saturday 30 May

Midsummer's almost here – the air was warm, bright and still this morning. Les and I cycled to the Inverurie shops. Ferns were uncurling along the roadside, speedwells and milkmaids strewn through new grass, broom bushes a blaze of gold. Peewits strutted across a stony field and a skylark hovered high above. What a song!

I hoped we wouldn't be overtaken by friends from the village. I still feel awkward when they drive past, en route to town. This time I cycled up the long hill home without getting off to push. I felt secretly pleased with myself. And to think, this time last year it was a struggle even to walk upstairs. I take my health and independence for granted again now, but the long pedal up that hill was a valuable reminder. Two cars passed us. Passengers waved and smiled. Complete strangers!

We were nearly home. Just a long, easy downhill slope, a sharp bend, and then the final stretch. I found myself responding deeply to the beauty of this quiet countryside.

'Don't think there's anywhere else in the whole world I'd rather be this morning!' I called out to Les as we pedalled along the last lane.

This afternoon the youngsters were in a playful mood. Murray unwound the long hose and showered everything in sight. He was hoping to turn the pressure up to full force and play the water jet right over the house, on to the pavement beyond.

'Don't you dare!' Les cried. 'You could soak the passers-by. Give those roses a good dousing instead.'

Murray did so, but managed to spray Rachel's almost-dry washing in the process.

'You did it deliberately,' she accused, eyes

flashing in anger.

There was a puddle of water inside, too. The electric kettle had leaked on to the kitchen work-space.

'Not again,' said Les. 'It seems incurably incontinent.'

I reminded him that the last small lump of 'blu-tack' had lasted almost six months. We can't complain at that. He tried the same remedy again!

Rachel was draped over the sun-lounger on the lawn, studying career brochures.

'I think I will try radiography training, after all,' she told us. 'Seems interesting. The pay's quite good. And I'd always get a job, too, wouldn't I Dad?'

I've been noticing how all the senior school youngsters are extra-concerned about work prospects now.

'Should do,' Les said. 'But don't forget that means another year at school and hard work on your physics.'

'All right, all right!' she grumbled. 'You've told me that a thousand times.'

Murray went to the local school fair this afternoon. He won a goldfish. 'Captain Haddock' was soon swimming round the glass mixing-bowl. The cat was full of disdain.

I glanced through the household accounts this evening. We're managing to keep within budget most weeks. The financial gain from not running the car is already apparent. We should be able to pay next month's quarterly bills without dipping into savings. Stuart's school fees are due to be increased, but not till September.

'I certainly hope to have work by *then*!' Les commented.

'It seems ages since you had that driving job interview. When will you hear the result?' I asked.

'I won't now. They've obviously filled the post,' Les said. I caught that 'what's-the-use' note in his voice again.

'Does that leave anything in the pipeline?'

'No, except the Dakota ferry-flight. Still very indefinite of course, and anyway it's not a job.'

He got up and fetched a couple of newspaper cuttings.

'I might write in response to these adverts,' he said. 'One's wanting a supervisor for personnel movements to and from the oil rigs, and the other opening is an office job with a transport company.'

'No harm in trying!'

Month 17

Monday 1 June (local public holiday)
A hot summer's day. I even shed my winter jerseys.
Rachel's been out on the lawn soaking up the sun;
Murray trying to catch trout; Les busy helping with
house renovations near by. He brought home a
gigantic plant of rhubarb this evening. We used some
and shared some, then Les dug a large crater beyond
the back fence and buried the rest, stamping those
long bulbous roots deep into the ground.

'There's sure to be a resurrection!' I told him.
'Rhubarb never admits defeat.'

Captain Haddock looked sickly tonight – so
pathetic, drifting in lop-sided fashion around the
bottom of his bowl. His tail is diseased, so we added a
little salt to the water – on the library book's advice.
Murray gave his fish a last sad look before bed. 'Do
you think he's going to get better?'

'Poor Haddock's breathing his last,' Les reported
at 10 p.m. 'Let's tip him out into the river.'

It was still quite light outside. The cat
accompanied us to the funeral, leaping over clover
clumps in a happy, cattish way. 'Captain Haddock
was buried at sea,' we'll tell Murray tomorrow.

'Crazy, isn't it?' Les said as we walked back,
enjoying the scent of broom from the riverside
bushes.

'What?'

'Murray fishing for trout this morning, then grieving over Haddock's imminent death this evening!'

Thursday 4 June

Nothing at all on the job front. We're awaiting replies from two local groups recently contacted. Les wrote to the Canada relatives. He's heard flying prospects are good there. Would we need visas? Are work permits hard to obtain? Red tape might rule out the whole idea. No harm in trying, though. Les is obviously forcing himself to fight this unemployment problem. The temptation to give in is so much stronger now.

Rachel, just in from school, saw the official-looking envelope which arrived for 'Miss R. Brown' in today's post. Scanned the contents. Her face lit up.

'Great!'

'What?'

'I've got a summer job! One up on you, Dad!'

This is the last of six holiday centres she's tried. 'Yes, please come. We need help,' they've said. Every other reply was a clear-cut 'No'. Vacancies already filled. Rachel's thrilled. She got out the map to locate Glencoe, then began to write out a clothes' list. I'm so glad for her. It will be hard work, but an interesting experience. She'll grow up a lot this summer.

Choosing and parcelling up a birthday gift for Jen has given me such pleasure today. She'll probably write back and say, 'You shouldn't have ...' But I should. I must! It gives such joy.

Friday 5 June

The phone rang at 11 a.m. Stuart's school. He'd had a "turn". Could we collect him as soon as possible? Les was out at Parkhill. I telephoned and he returned straight away. How could we fetch Stuart? Buses were too infrequent and not comfortable if he was feeling ill. A taxi?

'But they're so expensive,' I reminded Les. '£10 at least.'

We stood in the hall, trying to think quickly and clearly.

'I hate to ask the Grants, but they did offer their car any time,' Les remembered. 'The insurance cover is all right, too.'

I could see he was torn between the need to get Stuart home, and the awkwardness of asking for transport.

'I think you should ask,' I insisted. 'They'd be glad to provide help in the circumstances.'

Les was soon on his way to Aberdeen. I continued with my writing project. It helped keep my mind occupied. They were back by 1.15. Stuart was pale but cheerful.

'What happened lad?'

'Suddenly found I couldn't breathe. It was awful.'

'Had anything happened just beforehand? Or was the room hot?'

'No. Everything was quite ordinary and normal. Just came on all of a sudden.' It must have been similar to the previous incident – not nearly so alarming though. Stuart didn't become unconscious. He seemed hungry, and joined us for lunch. Then he fetched his latest model boat – it was holed at the last launching, so needs extensive repair.

I decided not to call the doctor. Stuart seems well again now. I'll make an appointment next week, and discuss the incident then. I doubt if anything could or should be done.

Thursday 11 June

Stuart is back at school, lively as ever. I talked with the doctor this morning. It seems the lad must have had a recurrence of that heart-beat irregularity, leading to breathing difficulties.

'Nothing can be done about it, and there's no need for restrictions or treatment,' the doctor reassured me. 'If another mild attack occurs just lie him down for a while, but if his colour changes get him to a hospital as fast as possible.' I do hope the problem won't recur.

I collected *Flight* on the way home. Les scanned the adverts as soon as I got back.

'Anything going?'

'One job only.'

'What?'

'Twin-Otter flying in the Antarctic!'

There were two letters this morning – from friends in England. Each contained £50. I sat looking at those cheques for a few moments, amazed at such kindness. The two ladies – retired now – gave similar instructions: 'Please use this money for treats, or for "gear" the children specially want, in order to be like their friends.'

The youngsters will be so pleased! Rachel can order some of those clothes in the catalogue after all, just in time for her holiday working-trip. Stuart is longing for blue jeans, and Murray keeps pleading for games 'trainers'. It will be good to be able to buy these items for them now!

We shared the news of the gifts at supper-time. The youngsters were wide-eyed, and full of excited spending-plans.

'Don't forget it's for treats, Mum,' Rachel reminded me. 'Not for buying boring things like toothpaste and cabbages.'

'Let's thank God together,' Les suggested, as we began our usual prayer time. I'm so glad the youngsters will have this clear evidence of God's care through others to store away as a valuable memory.

The phone rang while we were washing supper dishes. The McKays from Stonehaven. Would we like to stay in their home while they're away on holiday next month? Would we! It's a tremendous offer – it means we can have a summer break like most other families. No need to feel awkward now when people ask, 'Where are you going for your holiday?'

'To the coast!' we'll be able to tell them. And Stonehaven too, with its fascinating harbour, stretch of beach, swimming-pool, castle ... Yes, we'll be more than glad to accept so thoughtful an offer. Just wait till the boys hear!

'We could go on to Perthshire afterwards and visit the aunts for a weekend, too,' Les suggested, warming to the sudden prospect of a holiday.

'We were all excited this evening. School finishes in less than a month. By then my writing project should be complete. It will be a real holiday — except that there may not be work to come back to.

After supper, friends called to collect Stuart. He's off to the school play in Aberdeen. I'm glad he can go. Evening trips to the city are impossible now we're not mobile.

'But I *must* go to the school play,' Stuart protested last week.

'How? We can't get you there.'

His face dropped. Staff had been insisting that he must attend. Stuart was much too embarrassed to say we hadn't a car. But now he *is* going after all! Those friends don't know how much it means to Stuart to be just like all the other boys in his class. 'Don't worry, I'll certainly thank them for the lift!' Stuart called, as he hurried out of the front door.

Saturday 13 June

Sports Day at Stuart's school. It was cold, wet and miserable all morning. I had time to buy the twin's birthday gifts in Aberdeen before the events began (they're fourteen on Monday). It was fun to choose a calculator for Stuart, a digital watch for Murray. What a thrill they'll get! We've used some of the treat money.

Sports Day was celebrated beneath a canopy of umbrellas. Stuart's 800 metre race was third on the programme. I didn't dare tell him I'd got butterflies! I hoped he'd make it round the course. Great excitement as the starting-gun banged, and eleven lads sprinted off. Stuart ran well. He came in fourth. 'Well done, lad! Now, where's the tea tent?' I was glad to get out of that rain.

Home again, and I was frying sausages for tea when the phone rang. Edwin, from Vancouver.

'Great to hear you!' said Les.

Edwin crammed information into the next three minutes. Flying prospects are good - 'Come over and see!'

Les mentioned the possible ferry-flight. He'll contact Edwin as soon as he knows more on this. It was good of his brother to call. It's really been an encouragement. No time to ask about necessary red tape, though.

'We'll find out about that when we make the ferry plans,' Les said.

Monday 15 June

'Best Monday of the year, even if I do have to go to school!' Stuart smiled as both boys came into our room early this morning, eager to open their gifts.

'Wow, that's magic!' cried Stuart, pulling his calculator out of the box.

'Oh, a *digital*!' Murray beamed, trying to fit the man-sized band around his thin wrist. They couldn't wait to show their friends.

'That "treat" gift made it all possible!' I reminded them.

Rachel bought them two small goldfish. An appropriate replacement. The boys were very pleased. We all enjoyed a special tea this evening. Murray had squeezed a crowd of candles on to the cream-filled chocolate cake from the bakery. The boys opened a pile of cards. There were some generous money gifts, too.

'I'm even more rich now!' Murray announced.

I can't believe it's fourteen years since that bright June morning when, to our surprise, we ended up with two babies for the price of one. 'Still recovering from the shock!' Les says.

Tuesday 16 June

Glad to welcome the sun back. This afternoon I

watched a small boy walk by outside, carefully
carrying a tousled bunch of buttercups home to Mum.
Later, angry gulls swooped and screamed overhead
as a thieving crow made off with a hunk of our stale
bread and disappeared into a leafy beech tree. The
gulls, furious at being outwitted, glided off in loud
disgust.

'Let's sit out in the sun,' I suggested to Les. A
warm dry wind stirred the tall lupins and teased pale
petals from the strawberry blooms. It looks as if we'll
have a good crop this year!

But for all the brightness and beauty around,
Les's problems pressed heavily today. He sat staring
out over the river.

'I just don't seem to be getting anywhere. The
situation's hopeless. All my enquiries have come to
nothing. I'd have heard from those two local adverts
by now if they'd wanted me. As for anything
permanent in the flying line, it seems pointless even
trying. The competition's so keen that I'm pretty well
out of the running.'

I turned towards him, seeing that stricken look
in his eyes again. Les is reaching the end of his
endurance. Our breakthrough *must* come ...

'Hey, Dad, I'm going to thrash you at
badminton!' Rachel yelled, coming in at the back gate
from school. 'Get up you lazy old thing, and fetch
your racket!' There was a kindly 'I-want-to-cheer-you-
up' expression on her face.

'All right, all right. But please, only a short
game!' Les pleaded.

Saturday 20 June

Off to the Inverurie shops again this morning. Our
old car passed us in the village.

'It looks good and it seems to be running well!' I
called to Les.

The wind blew a rain shower our way, slowing
progress. Deep pink foxgloves are in bloom along the
laneside now, and tall grass-heads bent with seed.

As I pressed against the wind I was deep in

thought — much concerned for Les. Each day this
week has been a struggle. Today's mail brought a
letter from a stranger — Claire. (She's made contact
after reading a brief article I wrote on
unemployment.) Her husband has been out of work
for three months now; the going is rough and
bewildering. She told of 'getting married on a
shoestring four years ago' and of furniture for the
new home being 'old bits and pieces given by loving
friends - more precious than those bought by
ourselves because of their origin.'

Now their first baby is expected. Joy at the news
is tinged with uneasiness about future employment
prospects. 'I find it hard to go round our Mothercare
shop. I would love to buy so many things for the
baby. You're right about having really to learn to
"rejoice with those who rejoice" ... and yet I haven't
got too depressed about our situation. Between the
nasty little flashes of self-pity, resentment, and
unease, I feel that this is somehow a good time - a
pruning time, and growing time. Then a harvest? ... I
can see God doing beautiful things, drawing Andrew
and me even closer together, teaching us the value of
receiving from others, without our precious pride
being offended.'

Her letter echoed so much of what we feel. 'Do
you find it difficult really to share what's happening
with your friends?' (Yes! The longer the problem
drags on, the less inclined we've become to burden
others - we can't keep on giving unwelcome news.)
Claire continued, 'There's a real danger that
unemployment and tighter finances will isolate us
from others. To some extent we walk alone with God
... We want to learn to be content in whatever state
we are, but it costs, doesn't it? I suppose that shows
how valuable it is!'

How I warmed to that young couple. There's a
bond between us. At present, prolonged unemployment and its intense frustration isn't too
common round here. I hardly know of any close
friend in a similar position. People here look on our

family with particular concern. But it won't always be
so. Unemployment figures are steadily growing. One
day it will be an almost ordinary problem. Then
sympathy from the outside will inevitably be thinly-
spread, and the bond between those who suffer will
grow stronger. When, how, where will it all end?

The rain fell with steady force as we pedalled
back up the long hill. Cool against our hot faces. Not
unwelcome, though my damp slacks were beginning
to cling to my legs. I was determined this morning to
reach the top without stopping. The brow of the hill
was still out of sight, around a couple of bends. It
was a struggle, reminding me of the greater struggle
against the long slow, exhausting drag of
circumstance. There's no end in sight. We're weary in
the extreme. We're tempted to give up. If only God
would say 'three more weeks and then it will be over'.
That would make even the worst setback bearable,
easing the intensity of this wretched struggle. But
God is silent. He has chosen not to give details.
Why? The question has throbbed through my
mind so often. Why? . . . Les asks it, too. It goes on
and on. 'The answer to why? is often wait!' But we
can't wait. We're running out of staying power. We're
spent. We just want to give up.
But what about trust? Faith? Are they pointless,
too? Irrelevant? The Bible has a marvellous chapter
on faith (Hebrews 11). I remembered, when I read it,
discovering that trust can *win* whatever the
circumstances, because it *outlives* them.
'Through faith they fought,
    they did what was right . . .
    they were weak, but became strong . . .
    they were poor, persecuted, and ill-treated . . .
    they wandered like refugees . . .
What a record all these have won by their faith!'
Trust isn't always going to bring me what I
want. The chapter clearly shows that. It's not
necessarily a means by which I'll gain what I'm
asking from God. It is altogether richer and more

valuable than that. A means to new power, even in the anguish of extreme disappointment. This must be the 'value' I've been looking for all along! Even, in some strange way, the breakthrough?

I'm beginning to see that this trust in God is what matters most of all, much more even than the solving of our unemployment problem - though this, too, will one day come to an end. And meanwhile, faith in God's complete rightness can enable us to live without the thing we've longed and hoped for. If we place our hand deliberately in his we are safe - whatever.

We're still in the midst of our difficulties, still without any certain sign of relief, still fighting against increasing odds. But the easing of our despair need not wait until we have an answer. The gift of faith offers a refuge *now!*

The long hill fell slowly away behind us, rain still slanting down. Les pedalled slowly up alongside, his hair dripping with rain.

'This hill's hard going today. Want to stop?'

I paused to catch my breath.

'No, let's go on. We'll make it!'